The Great Smoky Mountains National Park

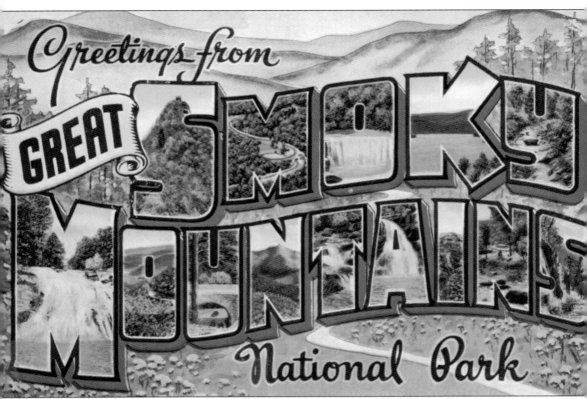

This postcard proclaims, "Greetings from Great Smoky Mountains National Park," with letters highlighting iconic views: S—Chimney Tops, M—The Loop, O—Cumberland Falls, K—Lake Santeetlah, Y—Little Pigeon River, M—Indian Creek Falls, O—Newfound Gap, U—The Loop near Newfound Gap, N—Mount Le Conte, T—Le Conte Creek, A—Abrams Falls, I—Charlies Bunion, N—Summer cottages on the Little River, S—Laurel Falls Trail. (Calvin M. McClung Historical Collection, Knox County Public Library.)

ON THE FRONT COVER: The resplendent view from Myrtle Point on Mount Le Conte recalls Henry Lix's observation: "The very beginning of the Great Smoky Mountains park idea appears to be as tenuous and vague as the rugged Smokies floating in a sea of shifting mist. Not one person, but a number of people, share the credit for originating kindred ideas separately." (Edouard E. Exline, Mark Pritcher Collection.)

ON THE BACK COVER: With the coming of Great Smoky Mountains National Park, many surrounding towns sought to take advantage of the influx of tourist dollars. Waynesville, North Carolina, positioned itself as the eastern entrance to the Smokies. The building in the background is the Haywood County Courthouse. (Great Smoky Mountains National Park Archives.)

POSTCARD HISTORY SERIES

The Great Smoky Mountains National Park

Adam H. Alfrey

ARCADIA
PUBLISHING

Copyright © 2012 by Adam H. Alfrey
ISBN 978-0-7385-9071-4

Published by Arcadia Publishing
Charleston, South Carolina

Printed in the United States of America

Library of Congress Control Number: 2012942262

For all general information contact Arcadia Publishing at:
Telephone 843-853-2070
Fax 843-853-0044
E-mail sales@arcadiapublishing.com
For customer service and orders:
Toll-Free 1-888-313-2665

Visit us on the Internet at www.arcadiapublishing.com

To my cherished wife, Olivia, and my inspirational daughter, Rose-Marie

CONTENTS

ACKNOWLEDGMENTS

The genesis of this book can be traced to 2009, when, amidst the 75th anniversary of Great Smoky Mountains National Park, I was honored to serve as curator for two exhibitions at the Museum of East Tennessee History in downtown Knoxville, Tennessee—*Pennies for the Park* and *Mountain Splendor*. Elements from these exhibitions along with the excellent work of scholars Christina Taylor Beard-Moose, Tim Hollis, C. Brenden Martin, and Daniel S. Pierce were important influences to the interpretation provided herein. It is my hope that readers will avail themselves of these and other authors listed in the bibliography. Of course, any errors in this volume should be ascribed to me.

I am also indebted to my colleagues Myretta Black, director, Knox County Public Library; Steve Cotham, manager, Calvin M. McClung Historical Collection, Knox County Public Library; the staff of the East Tennessee Historical Society, including director Cherel Henderson, curator of collections Michele MacDonald, curator of education Lisa Oakley, lunch partner Dan MacDonald, and interns Jessica Copeland and Nicole Barajas; and Myers E. Brown II, curator of extension services, Tennessee State Museum, Nashville, Tennessee. Thank you all for your encouragement and support, as well as for being patient sounding boards and conscientious reviewers.

To my family, Olivia and Rose-Marie, thank you for understanding the long nights and weekends spent on the project and for not protesting too much when I mumbled about postcards. Mom and dad, thank you for instilling in me an appreciation of things historical and for supporting me always.

And, finally, I certainly would be remiss if I did not recognize the individuals and the institutions that allowed me to peruse—and share—their postcard collections. Parenthetical courtesy lines consist of the photographer's name or studio, when known, followed by the collection in which the postcard resides: Buford and Barbara Blanton Collection (BBBC); Calvin M. McClung Historical Collection, Knox County Public Library (CMMHC); East Tennessee Historical Society Collection (ETHSC); Great Smoky Mountains National Park Archives (GSMNPA); Mark Pritcher Collection (MPC); Malcolm Rogers Collection (MRC); and author's collection (AC).

INTRODUCTION

When Horace Kephart resigned as director of the Mercantile Library in St. Louis, Missouri, *The Library Journal* of December 1903 reported his departure as "owing to ill health," explaining that he would soon "devote himself to literary work that will enable him to travel and be out of doors." By Christmas, Kephart's "ill health"—his troubling mental disposition, hankering for the bottle, and mounting financial woes—forced his wife, Laura, to resign, too, and return to her family's home in Ithaca, New York, with their six children in tow. Alone, searching for solace, direction, and a spark to ignite a literary career, Kephart yearned for, as he later wrote, "a Back of Beyond . . . a strange land and a people that had a charm of originality."

In late July or early August 1904, the eccentric librarian arrived in Western North Carolina's capital city, Asheville, but it would not be until November 2 that he would find his "Back of Beyond"—a two-room, log-and-plank cabin near the Everett Mines on Hazel Creek in the Great Smoky Mountains. Here, Kephart would fulfill his need to "realize the past in the present, seeing with [his] own eyes what life must have been to [his] pioneer ancestors." Here, he would meet a people who were "like figures taken from the old frontier histories and legends." Here, he would capture the information needed to write two books, which remained in print for decades—*Camping and Woodcraft* and *Our Southern Highlanders*.

For Kephart's health and career, the "mysterious realm" of the Smokies proved redemptive. Years later, when asked why he championed the establishment of Great Smoky Mountains National Park, he explained, "I owe my life to these mountains and I want them preserved that others may profit by them as I have." Kephart's nod to the saving powers of the mountains in the context of preservation was not new rhetoric. In fact, the first documented plea for a national park in Western North Carolina touted the mountains' healing potential. Dr. Henry O. Macy of Boston, Massachusetts, wrote to the United States Congress on October 29, 1885, "The pure air, water, and climate hold out a hopeful helpfulness to invalids from every land," a "value incalculable to millions yet unborn."

More intriguing, though, is the latter portion of Kephart's statement, his hope that the preservation of the Great Smoky Mountains would allow others to "profit by them as I have." Kephart did not wrest his profit from the mountains in the same manner as, say, the W.M. Ritter Lumber Company; its operations near Kephart's former campsite on Hazel Creek exported tangible assets—timber and dollars. Kephart's stock was considerably more nebulous, tied up in access to the "authentic." Without the land and the people of the Smokies, Kephart had nothing for sale—no veritable experience to sate his own curiosity or that of his readers.

Kephart tapped into what had been fueling the country's collective imagination since the second half of the 19th century—an emerging, distinctive regionalism and a need to reconstruct a national identity after the Civil War. "Amid the changes brought by immigration, industrialization, and urbanization," notes tourism scholar C. Brenden Martin, "Americans were eager to learn about the peculiar and exotic 'little corners' of the nation's rural backcountry." Through the pens of local color writers, such as Will Allen Dromgoole, the people and places of the Southern Highlands became just that—"peculiar and exotic." Among the most influential local color writers was Mary Noailles Murfree, who in 1884 penned *In the Tennessee Mountains*, followed a year later by *The Prophet of the Great Smoky Mountains*. "I do declar', it sets me plumb catawampus ter hev ter listen ter them blacksmiths, up yander ter thar shop," is how mountain residents sounded to Murfree's ear. A propensity to take up firearms in feuds and a predilection to distill and partake of a dram or two of moonshine was Murfree's idea of mountain behavior.

Murfree made her observations from a safe distance; she traveled into the mountains as a social elite, the only contact with the scruffy Tennessee mountaineers occurring on the fringes of the resort grounds of Beersheba Springs on the Cumberland Plateau and Montvale Springs in the Smokies. Kephart faults Murfree's superficiality in the opening paragraph of *Our Southern Highlanders*. A page later, though, he acquiesces, "Let us admit that there is just enough truth in [her] caricature to give it a point that will stick." He then follows, "Our typical mountaineer is lank, he is always unkempt, he is fond of toting a gun on his shoulder, and his curiosity about a stranger's name and business is promptly, though politely, out-spoken." Murfree pushes her description of the mountaineers to the extreme for effect. Kephart tries to temper such portrayal, but even the seasoned mountain writer ultimately admits, "We have a furtive liking for that sort of thing . . . an uncouth and fierce race of men, inhabiting a wild mountain region little known."

As Martin puts it, "Writers . . . focused on the most archaic aspects of life in the region because selling stories . . . required the specter of poor depraved hillbillies." But, "the specter of the hillbilly" was about to do more than sell books. A mid-1920s promotional booklet lobbying for the establishment of a national park in the Great Smoky Mountains heralds, "As inhabitants of the park, these picturesque Southern highlanders will be an asset, and so will their ancient log cabins, their foot-logs bridging streams, and their astonishing huge water wheels." Although the publisher, the Great Smoky Mountains Conservation Association, erroneously promises that mountain residents would "retain possession of their abodes within the park," the booklet accurately foretells that they—Kephart's contemporary ancestors and Murfree's gruff hillbillies—will become "objects of interest" to which "millions of tourists" would flock.

That by the 1920s, the promise of a regional tourism boom was being used as a selling point for the establishment of a new national park was an important development. For the first time, Americans—and, especially, East Tennesseans and Western North Carolinians—were thinking of national parks as an enterprise or, to borrow Kephart's phrasing, as a means to "profit by them."

The late-19th-century creation of national parks in the United States and their subsequent management were "haphazard at best," explains Daniel S. Pierce in his book *The Great Smokies: From Natural Habitat to National Park*. Land for the western parks, such as Yosemite, Yellowstone, and Sequoia, had been set aside, but reserved for what purpose? Some advocated for "utilitarian conservation," lobbying "to improve upon nature and harness it for more efficient human use," while others pushed for strict "scenic preservation," promoting Thoreauvian rhetoric and aesthetic sensibilities. Clarity to this left-brain/right-brain debate would not come until 1916, when Pres. Woodrow Wilson signed the National Park Service Act; therein, the purpose of the newly formed federal agency was defined: "To conserve the scenery and the natural and historic objects and the wild life therein and to provide for the enjoyment of the same in such manner as will leave them unimpaired for the enjoyment of future generations."

Enjoyment had certainly been interjected into the argument for national parks for some time. At a 1902 convention of the Appalachian National Park Association, for instance, one speaker reminded the Tennessee and North Carolina delegates that the future Great Smoky Mountains National Park "will unquestionably . . . become the nation's greatest pleasure ground, and if nothing more than this is to be accomplished in the perpetuation of these forests this is of itself more than sufficient." With the National Park Service Act, though, pleasure and preservation had become inextricably linked with the national parks' mission, and with the appointment of the deft and charismatic Stephen Mather as the service's first director, another "p" was about to be added to the equation—profit.

Mather, perhaps better than anyone else, recognized that his success as director hinged on the American people's perceived value of the national park system; to that end, he promised an administration "which shall develop to the highest degree of efficiency the resources of the national parks for the pleasure and profit of their owners, the people." For Mather, the business of the National Park Service was not only to tout scenic wonders but also to emphasize to communities surrounding national parks preservation's potential to develop a recurrent flow of dollars from pleasure-seeking tourists and the industries that support their travel.

Mather's sales pitch worked. Over the course of six years, beginning in 1916, annual visitation at the national parks in the West grew from 356,097 to 1,280,886. Regional boosters, especially those in the East, became increasingly envious of, and vocal about, the success enjoyed by the burgeoning—and thriving—resort towns near the western parks. In order to bridge this disparity, Mather announced his support for a national park east of the Mississippi River in 1923, and later that spring, the Southern Appalachian National Park Committee was formed to evaluate potential sites through a nonpolitical, nonpartisan process. For the first time, the reality of establishing a national park in the Great Smoky Mountains seemed a distinct possibility for East Tennesseans and Western North Carolinians. As Pierce words it, "Mather had given them the map to an El Dorado they always had known lay hidden in their mountains."

Significant progress toward the x that marked the mother lode occurred in the summer of 1923, when Ann Davis asked her husband, Willis P. Davis, "Why can't we have a national park in the Great Smoky Mountains? They are just as beautiful as these mountains." Her reference to "these mountains" pointed to the rugged, snowcapped peaks that she and her husband had just taken in on their tour of the western national parks. It is little wonder, then, that back in Knoxville, Tennessee, Willis Davis's first attempts to pitch the idea of a national park in the Smokies followed that comparison. Longtime park supporter and secretary of the Great Smoky Mountains Conservation Association Carlos C. Campbell recalled, "I was often irritated because I had to listen to [Davis] 'rave'—and that is what I then thought it amounted to—about the superlative beauty of the Great Smokies."

A more vehement rallying cry was needed, though, to sustain a successful park movement. Political maneuvering, interstate and intrastate rivalries, court battles, economic depression, and the strong personalities of movement leaders loomed as imposing challenges. Never mind the fact that the purchase of land posed, perhaps, that largest hurdle of all. By first estimates, $10 million was needed to procure 427,000 acres of land, 85 percent of which was held by 18 different lumber companies, the remainder being the private property of individuals, many with generations-long ties to their mountain homes. When the United States Congress initially decided that no federal funds would be earmarked to purchase land for the national park, booster groups from Tennessee and North Carolina committed themselves to raising $1 million by March 1, 1926. And to do so, they took a page directly from Mather's playbook.

In Tennessee, the de facto spokesman for the Great Smoky Mountain Conservation Association, Col. David C. Chapman, a veteran of the Spanish-American War and World War I, began espousing Mather-esque sound bites, promising "tourists by the thousands would pass through Knoxville to reach" this "veritable paradise of beauty." Other members of the association whose lineage was tied to the Knoxville Automobile Club and the Knoxville Chamber of Commerce drew attention to the park's geographic location near the major population centers of the East, many within a day's drive on roads that the *Knoxville Sentinel* extolls "would be built and maintained by the government, thus eliminating drawbacks offered motoring tourists." Boosters also drafted and trumpeted catchy campaign slogans. Some, such as "If you believe that it pays to attract tourists to Knoxville and Eastern Tennessee, help create a National Park in the Great Smokies!" appealed to economic sensibilities. Others, such as "Knoxville started the movement to establish a National Park in the Great Smokies, and Knoxville never started anything it couldn't finish!" prodded the community's resolve. In North Carolina, the pro-park organization Great Smoky Mountains Inc., under the leadership of Roger Miller and Horace Kephart, mounted a similar campaign, uniquely delivering its message from mountainous Marion to seaside Wilmington by way of a 24-car caravan.

After the dust settled from intense land negotiations and fortuitous fundraising, ranging from pennies pledged by school students to $5 million given by John D. Rockefeller Jr., Great Smoky Mountains National Park was established on June 15, 1934. It was now time to see if Mather's pleasure-and-profit model would hold true; that is, it was now time to see if millions would, in the words of park booster and automobile salesman Cowan Rodgers, "come through our gates and scatter the golden shekels in our midst."

When the National Park Service began working the land that would become Great Smoky Mountains National Park in the early 1930s, it was estimated that fewer than 200,000 tourists made their way into the mountains. By 1940, the year Pres. Franklin D. Roosevelt gave his September 2 speech dedicating the park "to the free people of America," that number had grown exponentially to 1,247,019. By 1950, Great Smoky Mountains National Park visitation exceeded two million.

One of those two-million-plus visitors was Edna, who on Sunday, June 4, 1950, sent a postcard of the iconic 6,593-foot Mount Le Conte from Gatlinburg, Tennessee, to Saint Paul, Minnesota. On the back, she wrote to the Luedtkes, "Heavenly days!! Beauty beyond words to express in this . . . Smoky Nat'l. Park. . . . Begin the 1,000 mile trip home tomorrow." Like the one Edna chose for her friends, early postcards of the Great Smoky Mountains often capitalized on the range's scenic grandeur. Issuing views that inspired and sustained the national park movement was a logical choice for publishers; they merely had to reproduce negatives that months earlier had been used to illustrate park booster propaganda. As the demand for new imagery increased, publishers continued with subjects that had already proved successful in selling the mountains to outsiders. Scenes of visitors taking in mountain hikes and contemplative vistas appealed to city dwellers seeking refuge in nature. Images of mountain residents, from the Cherokee of Qualla Boundary to the Walker sisters of Little Greenbrier, perpetuated the notion that progress had long passed by the mountains and called to those seeking to interact with the past. All the while, postcards advertising modern accommodations, fine Southern cooking, and easy-to-navigate roads tempted America's increasingly mobile middle class to get away from it all.

Thus, in many ways, the postcards of the Great Smoky Mountains are a visual representation of the arguments espoused during the grassroots campaign to establish the national park. More than that, these postcards serve as documentation of the warp-speed, radical changes a landscape undergoes when it is designated to become "an inexhaustible gold mine," and a "mecca for tourists." The call for preservation that first sounded in the Smokies at the turn of the 20th century brought lasting consequences, both positive and negative. Early on, Kephart recognized this impending dichotomy when he concluded, "Within two years we will have good roads into the Smokies, and then—well, then I'll get out." Today, the biodiversity preserved in Great Smoky Mountains National Park is only matched by the diversity of its more than nine million annual visitors and the complexity of the ever-encroaching development occurring along its boundaries. Scientists are just now beginning to understand the environmental impact of what it means to be the United States' most visited national park. Without a doubt, Kephart's 1904 description of the Great Smoky Mountains as "terra incognita" no longer applies. Rather, it is his statement, "I want them preserved that others may profit by them as I have," that remains apropos, as community leaders continue to search for the balance among preservation, pleasure, and profit.

One

THE SPECTER OF POOR DEPRAVED HILLBILLIES

For centuries, the Great Smoky Mountains have lured mankind. At first, the foothills were home to small communities of hunter-gatherers. With time, different groups rose and flourished. Native peoples were encountered by Spanish explorer Hernando de Soto in 1540, while searching for gold throughout the Southeast. Although similar European expeditions followed, it would be another two-and-a-half centuries before a new group of pioneering settlers would answer the Smokies' call.

Families with surnames such as Mingus, Hughes, and Enloe arrived in the 1790s and stayed in North Carolina's Oconaluftee Valley. By 1802, the Ogles and Reagans had made their way into Tennessee, settling in what would become Gatlinburg. Across the Great Smoky Mountains—from Cades Cove to Cataloochee and from Deep Creek to Sugarlands—other families soon joined. As good farmland was taken, newcomers moved up creeks and hollows.

These largely self-sufficient, self-contained communities sparked the curiosity of the social elite, a leisure crowd who came to the Smokies to mingle at resorts and commune with nature. Unable to grasp in short visits the broader range of mountain life, outsiders coined evocative terms, such as *hillbilly*, and perpetuated images of "lanky, sub-human creatures who were quick to feud, slow to work, and often indifferent to 'progress.'"

From far off, peering into the mountain communities, residents may have appeared isolated or unwilling to change. Outside observers, though, missed an important point: mountaineers had the unique advantage of being able to look out of the Smokies to see the larger world around them.

They lived much as rural people elsewhere. Their schools and churches were at the center of their communities. They traded with distant markets, driving teams of livestock and wagonloads of agricultural products to places hundreds of miles away. They worked to clear boulders and timber to build better roads. Their families sent their sons to fight in the nation's wars.

By the time the drama of establishing a national park began to unfold, the lure of the Smokies had assembled an interesting cast of characters, and they were all about to play unique roles.

From claiming to have killed 200 black bears in one year to having been given the honor of driving his oxen team across Knoxville's Henley Street Bridge during its opening ceremonies, Levi Trentham was, as one family member described him, "in a class all by himself." Larger-than-life mountain residents fueled the imaginations of local color writers, which may explain why this image of Trentham is captioned after Mary Noailles Murfree's 1885 novel, *The Prophet of the Great Smoky Mountains*. (Walter M. Cline, CMMHC.)

By 1910, when Robert L. Mason captured this image of Sam Burchfield holding his James Bean flintlock, terms such as *mountain white*, *highlander*, and *hillbilly* were used popularly to describe mountain residents. That same year, Burchfield was put on exhibit as a "veteran moonshiner" at the Appalachian Exposition held in Knoxville. (Robert L. Mason, BBBC.)

Cultural stereotypes perpetuated about mountain residents were often the result of sweeping generalizations. Author Horace Kephart—who likely took in this view of the Smokies from Bryson City, North Carolina—set out to define "Southern Highlanders" by immersing himself in their lives. Even with the purest of intentions, Kephart defaulted to blanket phrases. "Among them there is one definite type that predominates," observes Kephart, "Our average mountaineer is lean, inquisitive, shrewd." (AC.)

Of the stories Kephart recorded, among the most memorable were those of moonshiners, such as "Quill" Rose and his nemesis, revenuer W. W. Thomason. This image of a still in operation was taken by Japanese American photographer George Masa. Kephart and Masa were close friends, and both played instrumental roles in the campaign to establish Great Smoky Mountains National Park. (George Masa, CMMHC.)

As time passed, focusing on eccentric aspects of mountain life propagated the mythic hillbilly. For instance, this postcard of W.M. "Black Bill" Walker and his wife, Nancy Caylor, rightly acknowledges their pioneering spirit, having settled Walker Valley in 1859, at ages 21 and 19, respectively. Black Bill, though, continues to be best remembered for expertly wielding his six-foot rifle, "Old Death," and for fathering 27 children by multiple women. (Walter M. Cline, MPC.)

When family and neighbors banged pots and pans, sang boisterously, and processed in a post-wedding celebration known as a shivaree, the intent was to toast—and roast—the bride and groom. Outsiders misinterpreted the custom as proof that mountain residents lacked decorum and possessed a natural inclination to rabble rouse. (Walter M. Cline, CMMHC.)

AN OLD PHOTOGRAPH OF AN OLD TIME MOUNTAIN "MOONSHINE" STILL

With the so-called Moonshine Wars of the late 1860s and early 1870s and the coming of national prohibition in the 1920s, the traditional practice of moonshining took on a whole new hagiography. Emphasis was placed not on moonshine's roots in the British Isles, its medicinal use, or its role in the economy of subsistence farmers but on engrossing tales of hillbilly distillers, white lightning, and scrapes with the law. (Walter M. Cline, CMMHC.)

Sugarland Mt. from Gatlinburg.
© J.H. 2 Mt LeConte Series.

Finding the pulse of mountain communities was not easy. Later chroniclers would fondly recall scenes, like this view of Sugarland Mountain from Gatlinburg, and deem them bucolic, even Edenic. Not backwards hillbilly, not paradisial enclaves, mountain communities most often approximated historian Durwood Dunn's description of Cades Cove: "They were . . . representative of the broad mainstream of 19th- and 20th-century American culture from whence they came." (Jack Huff, BBBC.)

Families across the Smokies recognized the scrutiny their mountain home was receiving. One can all but imagine the couple pictured above, sitting on the porch of their Little Greenbrier home and echoing the words of another longtime resident interviewed by Laura Thornborough: "I'm tired of being writ up by these writer folks who . . . slip up on you with a Kodak when you ain't lookin' and go back and print it along with a lot of stuff about poor, primitive mountaineers." Peering out over a steep, cultivated hillside similar to the one pictured below, he concluded, "I'd like to see 'em try to use their new-fangled machinery on that field." (Above, CMMHC; below, Louis E. Jones, CMMHC.)

Springtime in the Smokies
© L.E.J. No. 23 Great Smoky Mtn. Series

16

The notion that mountain communities were self-sufficient may have been promoted by scenes, such as this one, wherein Tom (holding mallet and frow) and Jerry Hearon are in the process of riving boards for wooden shingles, known as shakes. Families did rely on the land, but they also participated in an active economy, buying and bartering at local stores and exporting ginseng, tanbark, cattle, hogs, and other goods to market. (MPC.)

RIVING BOARDS
(SHAKES)

A gun was one of a family's most prized possessions. It helped supply food for the table and defense from a host of dangers. It provided adventuresome tales shared by friends and neighbors. And, in the 1910s, the hunter's rifle also fueled a vigorous exchange of fox, mink, possum, and raccoon hides among fur traders and community members. (Walter M. Cline, MRC.)

OLD TIME MOUNTAINEERS
GREAT SMOKY MOUNTAINS

COPYRIGHT
W.M. CLINE
1-I-269

Raw goods were also processed in the mountains. On Mill (now Le Conte) Creek, 13 mills operated at one time, including the tub mill pictured here. Like many mill owners, Alfred Reagan of Roaring Fork charged a toll for his services, about one eighth of each bushel, whether that was corn, wheat, or another grain. Reagan was a diversified businessman, operating a blacksmith shop and a general store, too. (James E. Thompson, BBBC.)

Having wound carded wool into yarn throughout her life, Cades Cove resident Rhodie Abbott is seen here standing next to her spinning wheel, a familiar position. With the turn of the 20th century, handmade goods were, at times, replaced by purchased ones. For example, when Dorie Cope's husband took a cash-paying job in a lumber camp, she concluded, "For the first time . . . all this meant I could be as lazy as I wanted to be without feeling guilty." (AC.)

Dan Myers of Cades Cove stands next to bee gums, or hives, capped not with traditional mud but with what appear to be old boards, sheets of tin, and rocks. Hollow black gum logs also proved useful for long-term food storage. Families often sold or traded excess foodstuffs. The arrival of loggers and sawmill men provided ready buyers, more convenient than the distant markets. (AC.)

This postcard is humorously captioned, "Mountaineer's Speed Wagon." Nothing was speedy about the transportation of goods and livestock in the mountains. It could take two to three days to reach Maryville, Newport, or Knoxville and weeks to arrive at markets in Georgia and the Carolinas. Such trips afforded the opportunity to "return home not only with bolts of cloth and winter supplies of salt and coffee, but also with news and fresh experiences." (AC.)

CHURCH AND SCHOOL HOUSE
LITTLE GREENBRIER, TENN.

When the community of Little Greenbrier requested a school from Sevier County in the early 1880s, government officials offered to provide a teacher but not funds for a building. Tradition holds William "Gilbert" Abbott donated the land and Ephraim E. Ogle provided the logs. The teacher in this 1935 image is Herman Matthews, and Ernest Moore was the student responsible for the drawing on the blackboard. (Edouard E. Exline, CMMHC.)

The back of this postcard asks the reader to "write to the Board of Missions and Church Extension to see what you can do to help these barefooted mountain children at Pittman Center," which opened in Emerts Cove in 1920. Northern churches sent missionaries to needy mountain areas to establish churches, schools, and medical care. The services were often welcomed but not the unfair descriptions the missionaries sent home in order to increase donations. (CMMHC.)

Standing before the national convention gathered at Swarthmore, Pennsylvania, on June 28, 1910, Pi Beta Phi alumna Emma Harper Turner "outlined a plan for the establishment of . . . a settlement school in the Appalachian Mountains." After considering three sites in East Tennessee, the fraternity for women chose Gatlinburg. The settlement school's first instructor, Martha Hill, arrived in January 1912 and, two months later, began teaching in an abandoned schoolhouse. Initial classes were successful but small, so to test Gatlinburg's commitment, Pi Beta Phi issued an ultimatum: endorse the school by providing land or face withdrawal of the program. The community responded, and a new schoolhouse was built in 1914. As demand for programs increased, Pi Beta Phi's campus expanded. Teacher's cottages, like the one above, were added, as were instructional facilities, like the loom room below. (Both, AC.)

In describing the intent of the newly formed settlement school in Gatlinburg, Pi Beta Phi's newsletter, *Arrow*, states: "What we wish to do is to join in the effort to show them how to use their own resources, to develop industries suitable to their environment." Following suit of other settlement schools and in response to the national Arts and Crafts revival of the late 1800s, many of Pi Beta Phi's courses focused on traditional crafts, such as basket making (above) and fan making (below). Weaving and woodworking received special emphasis. Pi Beta Phi marketed these products outside the area as authentic mountain handicrafts. Sales helped fund the school, provided income for local crafters, and spread the image of the Great Smoky Mountains as a place where the past endured. (Both, Jack Huff, MPC.)

Two

A Veritable Paradise of Beauty

The Great Smoky Mountains had long supported towering stands of trees, described by Pres. Theodore Roosevelt in 1901 as "the heaviest and most beautiful hard-wood forests of the continent." Similar reports piqued the interest of lumber barons, and soon the mountains were filled with heavy machinery marked with company names, such as Little River, Montvale, Norwood, and Champion Fibre. Local men found jobs with these companies—for many, their first cash jobs—and spent their days lengthening rail lines deep into the mountain coves, felling trees, and skidding logs to mills.

Change had come to the Smokies, and some began to decry its effects. "Utter devastation" was how preservation-minded Paul Fink of Jonesborough, Tennessee, described the aftereffects of logging Balsam Mountain. Horace Kephart added his voice, calling Hazel Creek's denuded landscape "wrecked, ruined, desecrated, turned into a thousand rubbish heaps, utterly vile and mean." An awakening to the need to protect the environmental beauty of the Smokies was slowly entering the region's consciousness.

Scenic spots remained but were often reserved for those who sought them out, such as for the members of the Smoky Mountains Hiking Club. By the mid-1920s, proponents of Great Smoky Mountains National Park realized it was important to expose decision makers to the range's grandeur. The view from Mount Le Conte, for instance, moved then assistant director of the National Park Service Arno B. Cammerer to conclude the scenery was "of such supreme character, nationally instead of locally considered, that it will measure from every standpoint up to the best in our national park system."

At times, though, it was necessary to sell the Smokies' splendor to outsiders, so park boosters sent as envoys the images of local photographers, such as James E. "Jim" Thompson and George Masa. In time, many of these photographs were printed as postcards (visual calling cards for the mountains, as it were) and mailed across the country. As the rallying cry "Y'all come to the Smokies!" became stronger, so did the opportunity to develop a new type of renewable resource—tourists' wallets.

As early as the 1830s, wealthy lowlanders, oppressed by the summer's "bad air," began retreating into the Smokies in search for "the cure." Accommodations were provided at spa-like resorts, such as at the popular Montvale Springs. In that grand tradition, Kinzel Springs Hotel opened in 1914 on the banks of the Little River, offering guests access to two mineral springs, a dance pavilion, a tennis court, a croquet lawn, and horseback riding. (BBBC.)

A Smoky Mountain Home
L. E. J. No. 32 Great Smoky Mtn. Series

For visitors, mountain homes, perhaps like the one pictured here, also served as a night's accommodations. A columnist from Wilmington, Ohio, writing in 1900, planned his weeklong hike through the Smokies to strategically break at family homes. Ella Tipton Abbott recalled that her family reserved a "stranger bed" for itinerant lumbermen. Even as late as 1950, one couple wrote on the back of a postcard, "Invited into homes in every place, so haven't stayed in cabins at all." (Louis E. Jones, GSMNPA.)

24

Sclasser Leather Co., Walland, Tenn.

Hospitality could also be had at the inns and hotels found in company towns. The Schlosser Leather Company, pictured above, was charted in 1901 "to tan hides and manufacture leather." Located at Walland, a name derived from the company's principals, *Wal*ton and Eng*land*, the tannery benefitted from sitting downstream of the Little River Lumber Company. Supply of tannic bark was almost constant, and the junction of the Southern Railroad's Knoxville-Augusta spur with the Little River Railroad provided an efficient outlet for the 300 to 400 hides that were processed each day. In 1903, the plant's superintendent, A.J. Fisher, opened Chilhowee Inn to house visitors. The postcard below shows the inn's original structure and the later 16-room addition. (Above, MPC; below, CMMHC.)

CHILHOWEE INN, WALLAND TENN.

The full impact of tourism would not be realized until lumber barons, backed by well-heeled northern corporations, left their mark on the Smokies. One baron, Col. Wilson B. Townsend of Clearfield, Pennsylvania, founded the Little River Lumber Company, which laid 150 miles of rail lines to transport large hauls to its two-band lumber mill, pictured above. Even with advanced machinery, exhausting and dangerous work was required of hundreds of men, often local, to cut timber and snake logs down the mountain. To house this workforce and its increasingly cash-reliant lifestyle, company towns, some with as many as 1,000 inhabitants, popped up throughout the Smokies. Below is a 1909 view of the eponymous lumber village of Townsend. The sender of this postcard marked the hotel with an *x* and remarks, "This is where we get what we eat." (Above, MPC; below, CMMHC.)

Elkmont, Tenn. In the heart of the Smokies.

By 1908, the Little River Lumber Company had progressed deep into, as the postcard above notes, "the heart of the Smokies." In the lumber camp at Elkmont (above), the homes of workmen and foremen were parceled to each side of the railroad. "I told them I was living on the job and never got to see my wife in daylight," said Jess Cole, "I told them I was going to swap my bed for a lantern." In his book *Last Train to Elkmont*, Vic Weals adds, "Weekend drinking and fighting made the camps above Elkmont dangerous places to be." The lumber companies impacted lives; they also altered the landscape, as seen below. By the time the last tree was logged in the Smokies in 1939, an estimated two billion board feet of lumber had been exported. (Above, MPC; below, BBBC.)

Log Train in Smoky Mountains
Near Maryville Tenn.

Early on, Colonel Townsend recognized that only so many Little River trains, like the one powered by Baldwin Mallet No. 148 (above), could leave the Smokies before the timber was exhausted. Searching for a way to maximize his profit, Townsend struck on the idea of repurposing the lumber camp at Elkmont into a colony of summer cottages. So, in 1909, weekend-excursion trains were organized to lure wealthy Knoxvillians to the mountains. After a two- to three-hour ride on the "Elkmont Special," seen below, passengers stepped off the train and were presented with a sales brochure, mapping the available plots of land. As historian Steve Cotham puts it, "Ironically, tourism and logging came to the Great Smoky Mountains on the same train, the Little River Railroad." (Above, MPC; below, CMMHC.)

At Elkmont, on the 50 acres above Jakes Creek deeded by Colonel Townsend in 1908, a clubhouse and hotel for the Appalachian Club (above) soon appeared. Cottages on individual lots were built through the 1920s, organized by names such as Society Hill, Daisy Town, and later Millionaire's Row. In 1914, the Wonderland Club took over operation of the community's other hotel (below). And although members of this club viewed those over at the Appalachian as rivals, they all agreed that Elkmont was the place to summer in the mountains. Townsend's plan "for the beautiful Elkmont country" worked, and others were taking note. "The success of Elkmont," says scholar Brenden Martin, "indicated to local residents that tourism could succeed in Gatlinburg, . . . the main gateway of what promised to be the nation's most popular tourist attraction—the Great Smoky Mountains National Park." (Both, MPC.)

THE WONDERLAND CLUB HOTEL

MOUNTAIN VIEW HOTEL
GATLINBURG TENN.

"God-fearing, hustling, successful, two-fisted regular guys," as historian Daniel Pierce describes them, may have fought the battle to establish Great Smoky Mountains National Park, but it was the Smokies—through their grandeur and beauty—that won the war. When it was necessary to influence decision makers, trips into the mountains often began and/or ended here, at the Mountain View Hotel in Gatlinburg. Built in 1916 by A.J. "Andy" Huff, the eight-room hotel was originally intended for buyers visiting Huff's lumber operation at Sugarlands. Due to its popularity, Huff expanded the hotel in 1924, adding more rooms and a large dining room. It was in that dining room, on the evening of August 6, 1924, that members of the Southern Appalachian National Park Committee prepared to make their first inspection trip. Naturalist Paul J. Adams later recalled, "We had eaten. The table had been cleared. We were settled down to a discussion of a new National Park somewhere in the Southeast. Most of us wanted it in the Great Smokies. Our job was to convince the committee members." (Jack Huff, GSMNPA.)

For novices, trips into the mountains often required guides, such as Bud Lowe (pictured). "A good guide is a necessary personage in the endless hills of the Smokies," observes Robert Mason in his book, *The Lure of the Smokies*. "These men are known to be dependable and resourceful, with a fair knowledge of woodcraft and of camping as well as of fishing and shooting." (BBBC.)

When the Southern Appalachian National Park Committee left the Mountain View Hotel for the summit of Mount Le Conte the following morning, Paul Adams, himself a guide, said, "There were nearly as many guides and helpers as there were others in the party." Wiley Oakley, known as the "Roamin' Man of the Mountains" and the "Will Rogers of the Smokies," led the procession from Cherokee Orchard. This postcard is signed by Oakley. (Louis E. Jones, BBBC.)

A Jack Huff Photograph

Above the Clouds on Myrtle Po

"We were small spectators, awe-struck by the vast, primitive, beauty of an extra-special Myrtle Point sunrise," said Paul Adams, after having camped overnight on Mount Le Conte with the Southern Appalachian National Park Committee. Russell W. Hanlon, secretary of the pro-park Great Smoky Mountain Conservation Association, told the *Knoxville Sentinel*, "Mount Le Conte was our big show. We had first thought of taking the national park commissioners on three other side trips, but we reached the conclusion later that it would be better to take them to the top of Mount Le Conte where they could at once see the best we had to offer. . . . [Cameramen] placed their tripods on the highest points of Mount Le Conte and took pictures of waterfalls, gorges, and all the natural beauties of the rugged fastness of Le Conte." Over the next 10 years, additional inspection trips and the espousal of persuasive arguments would be required to influence decision makers. But, on this August 1924 trip to the top, the Smokies made a good first impression. (Jack Huff, MPC.)

In May 1925, Paul Adams, Harry P. Ijams, and Albert F. Ganier conversed around a campfire atop Mount Le Conte, having completed a successful day of bird study. A suggestion was made that a permanent camp be established at the summit. Obstacles stood in the way—locating a spring, gaining permission from Champion Fibre Company (which owned the timber rights), and receiving approval of the Great Smoky Mountain Conservation Association. Adams cleared these hurdles and returned in mid-July, with a German police dog named Cumberland Jack by his side, to establish the camp, seen above. Adams operated the camp for almost a full year, hosting key supporters of the national park movement. In 1926, E.C. "Jack" Huff took over management of the camp and established Le Conte Lodge, pictured below. (Above, James E. Thompson, BBBC; below, Jack Huff, GSMNPA.)

Jack Huff, son of the Mountain View Hotel's owner, Andy Huff, captioned the above postcard, "The Highest Lodge in the East," reminding the viewer that hospitality is afforded at an elevation of 6,360 feet, 233 feet below Mount Le Conte's highest peak. At such high altitudes, weather conditions are noticeably different from lower elevations, with freezing temperatures occurring in all seasons. Snow, not unlike that pictured below, is common from late fall to early spring. Jack Huff, his wife, Pauline, and their family cared for Le Conte Lodge until 1960, when Herrick and Myrtle Brown began looking after it. The lodge remains in operation within the national park today, and the current owners continue the tradition of packing supplies up the mountain by animal, although a seasonal helicopter drop has been added. (Both, Jack Huff, MPC.)

Sunrise from Mt Le Conte
Great Smoky Mountains National Park.
Jack Huff Photo

For visitors to Le Conte Lodge, past or present, standing witness at Myrtle Point to the sun's ascent over the distant horizon is a rite of passage. Back at the lodge, the smell of country bacon and black coffee confirms belief in everything good. Many have tried to capture the experiences pictured here, but nothing replaces being in Mount Le Conte's presence. When Jack Huff's 90-year-old, semi-invalid mother, Martha, requested to see a sunset from the top, Jack strapped his mother into a special chair, placed her on his back, and hiked seven miles to the lodge. Bad weather set in, and Martha returned to Gatlinburg three days later. Even though she never saw that longed-for sunset on her trip, she must have concluded as Paul Adams did, "Le Conte to me is something special." (Both, Jack Huff, MPC.)

Cooking on Le Conte
A Jack Huff Photograph

Of course, the boundaries of the proposed national park encompassed other natural wonders equally resplendent as Mount Le Conte. To trumpet these scenic spots, boosters relied on the talents of the area's photographers. Even when these cameramen focused their lenses on the same subject, their artistic eye produced unique, nuanced views, as illustrated by the four real-photo postcards of Chimney Tops reproduced on this and the following page. By choosing to look up the West Prong of the Little Pigeon River, Jim Thompson captures a monumental scene of The Chimneys, as they swell from their base towards the heavens. Almost a mirror image of Thompson's, Jack Huff's photograph, below, conveys the mountain's permanence, hovering over the river as it makes its way toward Gatlinburg. (Left, James E. Thompson, BBBC; below, Jack Huff, AC.)

The Cherokee called it Duniskwa' lgun'yi, or "Gap of the Forked Antler." When frontiersman settled the area, the vertical mountain peaks reminded them of chimneys, and in time, the rock spires became known as Chimney Tops or sometimes just The Chimneys. Walter M. Cline Sr.'s 1936 photograph, at right, taken from the Newfound Gap Highway impresses on the viewer the mountain's scale. The summit of the tallest chimney is 4,755 feet. Cline's depiction of The Chimneys is almost clinical compared to Louis E. Jones' evocative image below. By allowing the moss-covered crag to dominate the foreground, Jones emphasizes the ethereal display occurring in the background and plays to the formation's timelessness. (Right, Walter M. Cline, BBBC; below, Louis E. Jones, CMMHC.)

Knoxville-based Jim Thompson worked as a professional photographer from 1902 until his retirement in 1963. In the 1920s, Jim and his younger brother, Robin, were among the photographers documenting the Great Smoky Mountains. Proponents of the park shared the Thompsons' photographs widely. Images such as the sweeping vista of Bull Head, above, or the serene depiction of Sharp Top (later Mount Cammerer, in honor of Arno B. Cammerer, director of the National Park Service, and his role in creating Great Smoky Mountains National Park), below, were reproduced in a variety of formats, from inclusion in Great Smoky Mountain Conservation Association publications to portfolios intended to influence legislators in Washington, DC. Thompson Photo Products, the family-run photography business that Jim started, continues today. (Above, James E. Thompson, MPC; below, James E. Thompson, CMMHC.)

On his first night in the Smokies, author and artist Robert Mason took in a sunset from Gregory Bald, pictured here by Jim Thompson, and later wrote, "No artist could paint it. To do so he would need to compete with the Master Painter using the heavens for a canvas, the sunset and rainbow for a palette, purple mists and winds out of the west for brushes." (James E. Thompson, GSMNPA.)

This Thompson photograph appears in a mid-1920s booster brochure above a caption written by North Carolina author and photographer Margaret Morley: "In the forest where rocks are hidden from view under a thick carpet of moss, your horse wades knee-deep in luscious ferns." "Just as it was before the New World was discovered" and "a botanist's paradise" were among the many justifications offered on behalf of the national park. (James E. Thompson, GSMNPA.)

Photographs, such as Jim Thompson's image of Mouse Creek Falls, allowed for poignant comparisons when printed next to images showing the lumber companies' wake: the "naked skeletons of former sylvan monarchs, sacrificed to feed industry that eats without thought for the moment." Today's trail to the falls follows an old railroad grade once used to haul timber to Crestmont, a lumber town near Big Creek. (James E. Thompson, CMMHC.)

"By all means let us have a national park," wrote Francis Lynde, "and let it be big enough . . . to accomplish the conserving object." For those who contributed largely to that realization, honor was given. Here, Thompson captures the second-highest peak, named for Swiss geographer Arnold H. Guyot, and the fourth-highest peak, named after Col. David Chapman, "father of Great Smoky Mountains National Park." (James E. Thompson, MPC.)

Mt Guyot & Mt Chapman.

One of the photographic formats for which Thompson Brothers was known was the panorama. The top panorama shows Mount Le Conte as seen from Cat Stairs, a parlous area on Greenbrier Pinnacle said to be traversed more easily by cat than human. The bottom panorama looks into Huggins Hell, the deep, mountain laurel- and rhododendron-lined recess between the Boulevard and Alum Cave Trails on Mount Le Conte. (Thompson Brothers, CMMHC.)

This Thompson Brothers photograph compares the appearance of Rainbow Falls during summer and winter. Paul Adams served as guide when the Thompsons photographed the falls in December 1925. Adams recalled, "After many pictures were made of the frozen falls, Cumberland Jack and I started back to the top of [Mount Le Conte] and Jim and his crew, toward Knoxville." (Thompson Brothers, CMMHC.)

Le Conte Lodge operator Jack Huff was a prolific amateur photographer who, like the Thompson brothers, documented the grandeur of the Smokies. Shot with a box camera in the late 1920s through the early 1930s, Huff's photographs, especially the ones printed as postcards, were used to market the family's hospitality ventures. Huff's rich, moody images reveal a cameraman with lifelong, intimate knowledge of the mountains and range from detailed shots of mountain flora—such as the delicate bloom of the gnarly mountain laurel, above—to the celebrated views of the Smokies—such as the grand, snowcapped view of Greenbrier Pinnacle, below. Greenbrier takes its name from a leafy, thorny climbing vine, alternately referred to as carrion flower or saw brier. (Above, Jack Huff, AC; below, Jack Huff, GSMNPA.)

A little less than three miles up today's Rainbow Falls Trail, one takes in this view of the 80-foot-high falls, a view Jack Huff no doubt saw many times on his trips to and from Le Conte Lodge. In the summer, hikers can walk behind the spray, and if they wait for the afternoon sun, the rainbow for which the falls are named can be seen. (Jack Huff, AC.)

Here, Huff captures a man and his dog dwarfed by Alum Cave, one of the most scenic spots on Mount Le Conte. In the 1830s, the Epsom Salts Manufacturing Company made an effort to extract minerals from the site for medicinal purposes. During the Civil War, the area fell to Confederate control, and Col. William H. Thomas and his Cherokee troops mined for ingredients required to make gunpowder. (Jack Huff, BBBC.)

In the 1930s, Edouard E. Exline worked for the Civilian Conservation Corps (CCC) as a landscape architect and photographer. Apparently, photography was also Exline's avocation, as a number of non-CCC-generated images were reproduced as real-photo postcards. Exline's work is instantly recognizable by its clarity and high degree of contrast. Note the way Exline captures the interplay of sun and cloud (above) draping Mount Le Conte, the third-highest peak in the Smokies, and (below) the remarkable detail in the evergreen spruce-fir forest seen from Clingmans Dome Road. A contemporary of Exline was photographer Charles S. Grossman, who cared for the park service's cultural preservation program. Both men were interested in documenting mountain culture; their work is preserved today by Great Smoky Mountains National Park Archives. (Above, Edouard E. Exline, BBBC; below, Edouard E. Exline, CMMHC.)

Three

TO THE FREE
PEOPLE OF AMERICA

During the citizen-led campaign to establish Great Smoky Mountains National Park, promises of a "modern combination of Aladdin's Wonderful Lamp, the touch of Midas, the Magic Urn, and the weaving of straw into gold by Rumpelstiltskin" had been made. So, as the park prepared to hang its open-for-business sign, watchful eyes focused on the area's roads in anticipation of the influx of gold that would arrive in the passenger seats of Detroit's best.

When the park's first superintendent, Maj. J. Ross Eakin, arrived in early 1931, accessibility of tourists was likely the least of his concerns, as he and his staff were pressed to mark boundaries, prevent hunting, and fight and forestall fires. Two years passed, and improvements to park infrastructure came from an unlikely, yet timely, source—the Civilian Conservation Corps (CCC), a program of Pres. Franklin D. Roosevelt's New Deal legislation. Beginning in 1933 and lasting nine years, 23 CCC camps of approximately 200 men each were set up. Enrollees laid hundreds of miles of roads, cleared hiking trails, and constructed administrative buildings, fire towers, and campgrounds. They also participated in conservation work, planting trees and restocking streams with trout.

With the road having been paved, auto touring of Great Smoky Mountains National Park became a favorite pastime of restless families eager to see America. "A tourist is a person who drives 500 miles to get a picture of his wife standing by his car," Carlos Campbell rightly surmises in *Memories of Old Smoky*, as most seldom strayed far from their Chevrolets and Fords, settling to take in nature from a scenic overlook or a chance sighting of a black bear. The empowering view from Chimney Tops or the opportunity to be overwhelmed by Alum Cave was reserved for those who chose to know the Smokies more intimately.

Park rangers and out-of-towners now enlivened landscapes once inhabited by some 4,000 residents of the Smokies. Most had sold their land outright and moved off. Others opted for less money and lifetime leases. A few fought for the right to stay. How to interpret the contributions and legacy of these mountain residents became Great Smoky Mountains National Park's next challenge.

During the early 20th century, adventurous drivers guided their automobiles through the mountains on roads that were little more than two mud ruts. The routes often followed paths originally carved for wagons and cattle, such as at Indian Gap, where Paul Adams recalled seeing Model T tracks as early as 1923. Early mountain motorists also took advantage of cleared logging grades. (BBBC.)

Big Rock on Scenic Loop
Great Smoky Mountains National Park

Called the "back bone . . . of the road system" and praised for being "paved the entire route," the 100-mile Scenic Loop Highway began in Knoxville, passed through Maryville and Townsend, followed the Little River through the park area, and returned back to Knoxville via Gatlinburg, Pigeon Forge, and Sevierville. Here, a motoring couple pauses their tour for a picture in front of Great Stone Face. (Jack Huff, CMMHC.)

Prior to World War I, the justification for improved roads in the South hinged on providing rural farmers access to large markets. As automobile prices became more affordable and Americans turned to leisure travel, both Good Roads Movement leaders and proponents of the national park hit on a new rationale: Tennessee and North Carolina can "get rich quick" by entertaining tourists. They were right. In 1947, for example, an estimated 362,445 vehicles entered Great Smoky Mountains National Park and left behind an economic impact of almost $11 million. Touring the Smokies by car quickly became a national rite, and today, the ride to Newfound Gap remains ever popular. Traveling north to south, one begins just outside Gatlinburg at the park's boundaries, above. Within two miles, park headquarters, pictured below, are passed on the right. (Above, CMMHC; below, Walter M. Cline, AC.)

Some call it the Over-the-Smokies Highway, others Newfound Gap Road, and some simply US 441. Whatever one calls this transmountain highway, the 4,000-foot climb toward the North Carolina–Tennessee state line starts gradually but then precipitates upward. In no time, one is passing Sugarland Mountain to the west, while catching glimpses of Bull Head, seen here, and Mount Le Conte to the east. (Walter M. Cline, AC.)

A number of scenic overlooks occur along US 441, and the one at mile four commemorates the ardent support Carlos Campbell gave to the national park movement. Campbell served as secretary of the Great Smoky Mountain Conservation Association for 20 years and later chronicled his experience in *Birth of a National Park*. A few moments after leaving the overlook, one takes in this view of Chimney Tops. (Walter M. Cline, AC.)

Paul Fink's statement, "One will travel on his hands and knees many times in reaching some of these spots," aptly describes this pair's quest to reach the summit of The Chimneys. Such effort is rare for the majority of motoring tourists. In 1968, *National Geographic* dubbed Great Smoky Mountains National Park "drive-in nature," observing only six percent of visitors leave their cars and take to the trails. (GSMNPA.)

The reward for those willing to abandon the steering wheel is large. When author Michael Frome and his hiking companions John Morrell and Harvey Broome took in a similar view from Chimney Tops, he said, "It was a world for dreaming on the manifest mysteries, myths, marvels, and meanings of the Great Smoky Mountains. . . . Quiet for a time were the three of us, the older eyes perceiving far more than mine." (Walter M. Cline, CMMHC.)

Upon entering the first of two tunnels on Newfound Gap Road, one loses sight of Chimney Tops for just a brief moment. Civilian Conservation Corps (CCC) enrollees built both tunnels in the 1930s, and when the passages needed to be enlarged in the early 2000s, the road was lowered to preserve the CCC's intricate stonework, as seen above. Sight of The Chimneys is regained as one progresses around The Loop, where the highway crosses itself and launches automobiles toward Newfound Gap. The Loop, below, replaced a series of four narrow switchbacks. Such engineering provided tourism advocates the opportunity to herald the ease of modern driving in the mountains. Drivers, for example, were often promised they could maintain the same gear throughout their entire trip to the "rooftop of America." (Both, Walter M. Cline, AC.)

Above, tourists, having just made use of the "ample room for parking hundreds of cars," congregate on the Laura Spelman Rockefeller Memorial to take in views of both Tennessee and North Carolina. Newfound Gap, elevation 5,045 feet, was so named since it replaced a passage first cut in the 1830s at Indian Gap, two miles west. As the postcard below demonstrates, the Newfound Gap parking area provides visitors with a number of choices. One could choose to motor on through the Oconaluftee Valley into Cherokee, North Carolina, or retrace his path and return to Gatlinburg, Tennessee. One could choose to hike along the trail to Mount Kephart and Mount Le Conte (now the Appalachian Trail). Or, one could choose the drive to Clingmans Dome. (Above, James E. Thompson, CMMHC; below, Walter M. Cline, AC.)

On January 23, 1928, John D. Rockefeller Jr. offered $5 million to the national park's cause. To test the resolve of the campaign, Rockefeller's gift required the equal matching of funds. In the end, efforts proved successful, and as the memorial at Newfound Gap (above) reads, "For the permanent enjoyment of the people, this park was given one half by the peoples and states of North Carolina and Tennessee and by the United States of America and one half in memory of Laura Spelman Rockefeller by the Laura Spelman Rockefeller Memorial founded by her husband John D. Rockefeller." Officially established on June 15, 1934, Great Smoky Mountains National Park was not dedicated until September 2, 1940, when Pres. Franklin D. Roosevelt stood at the Laura Spelman Rockefeller Memorial (below) and said in part: "Here in the Great Smokies we have come together to dedicate these mountains and streams and forests . . . for the service of the millions of American people." (Above, Walter M. Cline, AC; below, CMMHC.)

Clingmans Dome Road, sometimes called The Skyway, peels off at Newfound Gap and reaches elevations of about 6,300 feet, making it the highest paved road in eastern America. Early park planners and boosters, envious of Shenandoah National Park's skyline drive, lobbied for a much longer crest-line road than today's seven-mile spur, seen here. Vocal opposition to "the noise and impact of the machine world" came from Harvey Broome, as an individual first, and later as a founder of the Wilderness Society. In 1935, Secretary of the Interior Harold Ickes settled the debate: "This is an automobile age, but I do not have much patience with people whose idea of enjoying nature is dashing along a hard road at 50 or 60 miles per hour. . . . I do not happen to favor the scarring of a wonderful mountainside." (Both, Walter M. Cline, AC.)

Elevation 6642 feet.

From Clingmans Dome parking area, one could take in the view above, but to get the full effect, one had to climb another 332 feet to the summit, where the Civilian Conservation Corps built the wood-frame observation tower (left) in 1937. In describing the tower, the postcard erroneously lists Clingmans Dome's elevation as 6,642 feet, which is off by one foot. Those 12 inches would have mattered to Thomas Lanier Clingman, who in the mid-1800s, engaged in a public debate with Elisha Mitchell over which peak in the Black Mountains of North Carolina was the highest. The highest point in the East, 6,648 feet, was eventually named in Mitchell's honor. Smoky Dome, highest peak in the Smokies and third-highest in the East, became Clingmans, after he, guide Robert Collins, and Princeton professor Arnold Guyot charted the grand mountain in 1858. (Both, Walter M. Cline, AC.)

In 1960, a 45-foot concrete observation deck, above, replaced the old wooden one atop Clingmans Dome. The modern tower's circular design emphasizes the 360-degree views afforded visitors, which on a clear day can extend up to 100 miles. Sadly, such views are rare, especially in the summer, as air pollution reduces visibility by up to 80 percent. Even the northern view of Mount Le Conte, below, is not the same as when this postcard was produced in the 1940s. In recent years, tiny insects called balsam woolly adelgids have attacked Fraser firs, vibrant and full in the postcard's foreground, and reduced them to dead, silvery spires. The National Park Service is currently searching for an effective means to control the spread of this nonnative adelgid. (Above, AC; below, Walter M. Cline, AC.)

In her book, *The Wild East*, Margaret Lynn Brown observes that "what really got people out of Gatlinburg and Cherokee was: bears." So, in short order, *Ursus americanus* became the furry, cute, Yogi Bear–esque mascot of the Smokies. In reality, black bears are shy yet powerful, with males weighing more than 200 pounds and standing about 6 feet tall. (George Barnes, CMMHC.)

100 lb. bear killed by B.G. Foster Gatlinburg, Tenn.

Great Smoky Mountains National Park provided the first real sanctuary for black bears. Mountain residents had hunted them hard, especially when livestock was threatened. Cataloochee resident G.N. "Turkey George" Palmer claimed to have killed so many bears he ordered a steel casket to protect his bones from vindictive bruins. Hunting continued outside the park, as shown here; poaching occurred inside. Some bears were captured and put on display in front of souvenir stands to bait tourists. (MRC.)

When motor tourists, like the ones above, caught sight of a bear, it instantly became the highlight of the trip. Cars were parked. Cameras were focused. And, food was often thrown to lure the animals closer. Ross Eakin, the park's first superintendent, carped, "The animals, now, apparently associate human beings with a potential and choice food supply." Such activity, although unlawful, was "a source of pleasure and amusement to the tourists," as the postcard above puts it. Bears saw it as an easy meal and quickly became proficient panhandlers. "Bear jams" ensued along park roads, sometimes tying up traffic for hours, as passengers, like the ones at right, foolishly abandoned cars for a closer look. Managing the interactions of humans and bears remains a high priority for the park service, and willfully approaching any distance that disturbs or displaces a bear remains illegal. (Above, BBBC; right, CMMHC.)

"I LIVE IN THE GREAT SMOKY MOUNTAINS NATIONAL PARK AND I AM LOOKING FOR A NUT. COME AND SEE ME SOMETIME" 1-I-180 ©COPYRIGHT W.M. CLINE

While black bears may be the star attraction, Great Smoky Mountains National Park is refuge to an additional 65 mammal species, more than 200 bird species, 50 native fish species, and 30 salamander species. The "nutty" gray squirrel pictured on this postcard proclaims, "I live in the Great Smoky Mountains National Park and I am looking for a nut. Come and see me sometime." (Walter M. Cline, BBBC.)

"Just as show windows serve to lure people into the store so are the park roads responsible for many tourists taking to the trails where they can enjoy more intimate contacts with the beauties of nature," reasons *Tennessee Wildlife*. Days spent hiking, camping, fishing, observing wild flowers, or studying wildlife left little time for sending correspondence back home, which made this postcard useful. (AC.)

Certainly, to enjoy nature one must be prepared, and camps in the Smokies sought to ready young ones. The 1924 annual for Camp Le Conte, a boys' summer camp at Elkmont (pictured), states, "Our purpose is to develop the boy in many ways for future citizenship through out-door life." At Camp Margaret Townsend, which opened in 1925 in nearby Walker Valley, Girl Scouts participated in similar learning. (MPC.)

Among the activities to first become popular in Great Smoky Mountains National Park were those already enjoyed at western parks, such as trout fishing. Much of the park's 2,115 miles of streams were adversely affected by logging. To accommodate eager fishermen, an aggressive restocking program was undertaken, which introduced nonnative game fish, such as rainbow and brown trout. As a result, native species—and particularly brook trout—suffered. Efforts continue to regain equilibrium. (CMMHC.)

BREAKFAST ON AN OVER NIGHT HIKE AT CAMP LE CONTE GATLINBURG, TENN.

Horseback riding was another borrowed western experience and a favorite activity among wealthy park backers. Overlooking the horses' impact on the Smokies, administrators catered to, as Margaret Lynn Brown puts it, the "primacy of the tourist," and 550 of the park's 817 miles of trails were opened to horse traffic. Since then, many have decried the muddy, smelly wake the horses leave behind. (CMMHC.)

Of course, not all recreation has detrimental effects on the environment, such as the summertime ritual of slipping into one of the Smokies' cool mountain streams for a refreshing swim. For her dip, this woman has chosen The Sinks, a swirling pool on the Little River created in 1896 when the England Lumber Company dynamited the riverbed to clear a logjam. (Walter M. Cline, CMMHC.)

Avid hikers in the Smokies have their favorite spots. Sometimes, these sites are prized for their remoteness. Others are preferred for the grand views they offer. And still others are recommended for their uniqueness, such as the two pictured here: Peregrine Peak, right, and Charlies Bunion, below. "Resembling Italy's Leaning Tower of Pisa," as Allen Coggins describes it, Peregrine Peak is located on the south side of Mount Le Conte, near Alum Cave. The peak gets its name from peregrine falcons, or duck hawks, as locals say, which nested here. Once eradicated from the park, peregrine falcons have been reintroduced in recent years. Originally called Fodderstack, the formation below received its name on a 1929 survey trip, when Horace Kephart said the eroded crag had the "appearance of Charlie Conner's bunion." (Right, CMMHC; below, Walter M. Cline, CMMHC.)

Above, hikers progress along the Appalachian Trail, having just passed Charlies Bunion along the Sawteeth Range. Often referred to simply as the "AT," the Appalachian Trail was planned by Benton MacKaye and remains the longest continuously marked footpath in the world, spanning 2,180 miles from Springer Mountain, Georgia, to Katahdin, Maine. Completed in 1937, the AT traverses the length of Great Smoky Mountains National Park for 72 miles, with 34 of those miles above 5,000 feet, the longest continuous height hikers face. About every 8 to 10 miles, shelters, like the one below at Double Spring Gap, are located on trail. Near the summit of Clingmans Dome, the Appalachian Trail intersects the Mountains-to-Sea Trail, which, when completed, will extend 900 miles through North Carolina to the Atlantic Ocean. (Above, Jack Huff, MRC; below, Walter M. Cline, CMMHC.)

Among the trails most utilized in the park are those that lead to waterfalls. The park service estimates 200,000 people a year trek to Laurel, Grotto, Rainbow, and Abrams Falls. This 1910s postcard depicts the rushing flow of Abrams Falls plummeting 20 feet into the pool below, the deepest in the park. The falls and creek are named for Old Abram, a Cherokee chief whose village stood west of Cades Cove. (CMMHC.)

One 1940s travel brochure describes the trail to Laurel Falls, above, this way: "The next trail . . . is the short hike to Laurel Falls. . . . Good views of surrounding mountains, impressive rock cliffs . . . and an exceptionally attractive double waterfall are main features. The trail crosses a wide ledge that separates the upper and lower falls. This trail is so good that it may be taken in high heels." (CMMHC.)

(c) T-22 Ramsey Cascades
in the Great Smoky Mountains National Park

The scale of waterfalls in Great Smokies National Park ranges from the torrential Ramsay Cascades (above) to the accumulative Place of a Thousand Drips (left). Ramsay Cascades, named after a family who settled near Cosby in the mid-1800s, is the tallest waterfall in the park, measuring 100 feet. Standing 80 feet high and 55 feet wide, Place of a Thousand Drips is so called for the countless diminutive streams that fall from Cliff Branch. Whereas Ramsay Cascade requires a rigorous climb, gaining 2,000 feet in elevation over four miles, Place of a Thousand Drips can be viewed from Roaring Fork Motor Nature Trail above Gatlinburg. Both falls are dependent on the abundant rain the Smokies receives, which on average is more than 85 inches per year. (Above, CMMHC; left, Clair Burket, CMMHC.)

The caption for the postcard above reads in part: "Quite a number of cabins in the park are still occupied—the owners having exercised their privilege to retain a life-time lease." No longer able to hunt or work their land, mountain residents who negotiated to stay within park boundaries became just another stop on the tour—an eventuality the five Walker sisters of Little Greenbrier realized all too well. In 1946, when *The Saturday Evening Post* ran an article about the sisters, visiting their home, pictured below, became a not-to-be-missed attraction. Seven years later, the two remaining Walker sisters beseeched the park service for help. "We are not able to do our work and receive so many visitors, and can't make sovioners [*sic*] to sell like we once did," they wrote. (Above, James E. Thompson, CMMHC; below, Walter M. Cline, CMMHC.)

For the National Park Service, preparing exhibitions of the Smokies' flora and fauna at visitor centers, such as at Sugarlands, seen here, was relatively straightforward when compared with the task of interpreting the legacy of the park's former residents. In 1938, a committee was appointed to define how the park would fulfill its mission "to conserve . . . historic objects." A decision was made to focus on pre-1890 pioneer culture. This played well to the image of contemporary ancestors that local color writers and park boosters had used in selling the Smokies. It also set up the opportunity for the mountain residents' removal story to be misinterpreted. The first writers to deal with the topic, like Laura Thornborough, often downplayed or trivialized relocation. Later, observers would paint the inhabitants so-called pioneer existence Edenic and their eviction savage, even violent. (Both, Walter M. Cline, CMMHC.)

So, as mountain residents moved off, structures left behind were auctioned off for dismantlement or burned if not salvageable. Only the "best examples of pioneer architecture" were retained, such as the home and barn of Noah "Bud" Ogle, pictured here. Ogle settled on 400 acres of farmland in White Oak Flats (now Gatlinburg) in 1879. Today, the Ogle farm is interpreted by way of a self-guided nature trail. (Walter M. Cline, CMMHC.)

In 1945, the farming community of Cades Cove, pictured, was designated a historical area, and plans were made to restore old structures, push back the encroaching forest, and remove, as historian Durwood Dunn puts it, "anything which might remotely suggest progress or advancement beyond the most primitive stages." The park service's interpretive plan worked. The back of this postcard states, "Sturdy log structures remain today as memorials to [the] pioneer way of life." (Walter M. Cline, CMMHC.)

The oldest log structure preserved in Cades Cove is this cabin, built by John Oliver in the 1820s. The interpretive brochure for the 11-mile scenic loop reads, "Not much except mules, muscles, simple tools and neighborly help was needed to fell the trees, get them to the building site and build the house. . . . Such a home sometimes served as a business, school, hospital, orphanage, nursing home or poor house." (Walter M. Cline, CMMHC.)

The Gregg-Cable House, seen here just beyond the sorghum mill, offers some evidence of Cades Cove's former status as a progressive mountain community. Built in 1879 by Leason Gregg, the home is believed to be the first all-frame house in Cades Cove. Gregg operated a store from the first floor, until selling it to siblings Dan and Rebecca Cable. Due to illness in Dan's family, "Aunt Becky" cared for the home and farm until age 96. (CMMHC.)

The Gregg-Cable House was relocated next to the Cable Mill (above), where the structures anchor a curated pioneer farmstead. Interpreters grind corn at the mill regularly and, from time to time, put on special demonstrations, such as boiling down pressed sorghum juice (below). Emphasis is placed on the subsistence aspects of farm life. Downplayed is the active community John W. Oliver, great-grandson of the first John Oliver, fought so vehemently to save when the park commission came calling for his land. As mail carrier, tourist lodge operator, and pastor of the Primitive Baptist Church, the fourth-generation Oliver likely surmised, as did Durwood Dunn, that his 600 or so Cades Cove neighbors were "ordinary, decent citizens who often acted collectively . . . to the enormous economic fluctuation, social change, and political disruption surrounding their lives." (Both, Walter M. Cline, CMMHC.)

Across the mountains in the Oconaluftee Valley near Cherokee, North Carolina, the National Park Service opened another interpretive site, the Pioneer Museum and Farmstead (above) in 1953. In her guidebook, *The Great Smoky Mountains*, Laura Thornborough compares the outdoor museum to Cades Cove, remarking it offers the same opportunity to "see how the mountain man lived and can admire his handiwork and inventive ingenuity." At what is known today as the Mountain Farm Museum, visitors are provided access to a farmhouse, barn, apple house, springhouse, blacksmith shop (below), and the nearby Mingus Mill. In all, Great Smoky Mountains National Park has preserved more than 90 structures inhabited or used by former residents. The best sites to see them remain Cades Cove, Cataloochee, Oconaluftee, and Roaring Fork Motor Nature Trail. (Above, BBBC; below, CMMHC.)

Four

OBJECTS OF INTEREST TO MILLIONS OF TOURISTS

Primed first by the descriptions of local color writers and sustained by the portrayal of the "wild frontier" in popular culture, sightseers from around the country arrived in the Great Smoky Mountains eager to interact with their contemporary ancestors— the "liquored-up hillbilly" and the "teepee-housed Indian."

Fearful of disappointing their clientele and knowing that, as Southern tourism expert Tim Hollis puts it, "trading on such popular caricature could be an easy—if somewhat guilty—road to riches," attractions popped up in the mountains, pandering to these popularized, and ingrained, cultural stereotypes. Gatlinburg's Homespun Valley Mountaineer Village, for example, was among the first to attract out-of-towners with the promise of witnessing "'a run' of corn likker."

Cultural paradoxes resulted. Take the transformation of Cherokee, North Carolina, as a case in point. Between 1875 and 1880, the Eastern Band of the Cherokee and the boundaries of their land trust were recognized by the United States. Tourism on the Qualla Boundary was limited until 1914, when the annual, crowd-drawing Cherokee Indian Fair commenced, showcasing traditional handicrafts and tribal culture. Other times of the year, though, the Cherokee, having withstood decades of forced assimilation, appeared to be "a standardized product not unlike the citizens of Iowa or Ohio."

That 1930 description by a newspaper columnist would change dramatically after World War II, as cars full of out-of-towners coasted down the Smokies either on US 441 or the Blue Ridge Parkway for a chance to see "real" Indians—real ones like they saw in Wild West television shows. Teepees never before seen in Cherokee were subsequently erected. Cherokee men donned the be-feathered costumes of Plains Indians and began "chiefing"—that is, standing in front of gift shops, offering photo opportunities in exchange for tips.

In time, this cultural misappropriation spurred the Cherokee Historical Association to develop three attractions—the outdoor drama *Unto These Hills*, the Oconaluftee Indian Village, and the Museum of the Cherokee Indian—that would "perpetuate the history and traditions of the Cherokee." Even then, entertainment value and other influences continued to trump historical accuracy, on occasion.

In the 1830s, Cherokee lands were blocking the progress of a growing nation and states. To make room, the federal government persuaded the Cherokee to sign the 1835 Treaty of New Echota, under which they agreed to move west within two years. When the Cherokee did not move, federal troops rousted them from their homes and held them in camps to await removal. Thus began the tragic Cherokee removal, known as the Trail of Tears. Some 20,000 Cherokees were forcibly moved, with only 16,000 making it to reserved lands out West. A handful of Cherokee in the East were able to evade removal, either through North Carolina's Reservation Act of 1819 or by ducking the US Army. For this band of Cherokee, the second half of the 1800s would prove to be a troublesome period, filled with intense land negotiations and attempts to gain recognition. Ultimately, the Qualla Boundary, a land trust of 56,000 aces, was established on the eastern edge of what would become Great Smoky Mountains National Park. And the town of Cherokee, as seen above in the early 1900s, became the park's southern gateway. (CMMHC.)

During the campaign to establish Great Smoky Mountains National Park, proximity to the Qualla Boundary had been an important selling point, and the Cherokee had proved early and important allies to the movement. In 1899, they sold 33,000 acres to the United States Department of the Interior for the purpose of creating a national park in the Smokies, banking that such a move would transform the "isolated, obscure Indian group into the most visited Native American group in the United States." The Cherokee were right, and before long, they found themselves adopting popularized Wild West stereotypes to appease visitors, eager to see teepees and feathers. As seen in the images here, pizzazz quickly became more important than historical accuracy. (Above, Walter M. Cline, AC; below, Walter M. Cline, CMMHC.)

CHIEF STANDING DEER CHEROKEE
INDIAN RESERVATION, N.C.
©CLINE
1-P-15

Although it is not certain who among the Cherokee was the first to appropriate a Plains Indian costume, there are telling early examples. In 1935, for instance, Goingback Chiltoskey is said to have dressed as a Sioux warrior, mounted a horse, and participated in a parade in downtown Asheville. "Chief" Carl Standingdeer, pictured here, was likely among the first to don an elaborate headdress and pose for photographs in exchange for tips, as the sender of this 1938 postcard readily admits, "We have just been talking to this Indian." The lucrative practice of engaging Kodak-toting visitors, known as "chiefing," became a mainstay on Cherokee's tourist strip, as more and more "chiefs" posted themselves in front of souvenir shops. In time, shop owners added additional pay-to-photograph props, such as stuffed black bears and teepees. "This isn't history, this is show business, and when you're in show business you have to dress the part," said longtime chiefing veteran Henry Lambert. (BBBC.)

Beginning in 1914, residents of the Qualla Boundary orchestrated an annual event, known as the Cherokee Indian Fair. Although intended more for the Cherokee than tourists, the festival did reach out to nearby neighbors, and given the number of reviews that appear in Knoxville's newspapers in the 1920s and 1930s, even out-of-state crowds found it to be a favorite fall destination. Most reporters remarked on the demonstration of traditional ways of life, such as grinding corn with mortar and pestle, seen at right. Others commented on the agricultural exhibits, recalling "every type of vegetable that can be made to grow in the North Carolina climate was shown." And, almost all mentioned the fair's centerpiece—the intense, muscular stickball tournament, seen in play below. (Right, GSMNPA; below, CMMHC.)

INDIAN WOMAN POUNDING CORN
CHEROKEE RESERVATION, N.C

In time, even the well-intended Cherokee Indian Fair succumbed to pressures of outsiders looking for Hollywood's Indians. Later postcards, such as these, show the addition of western war bonnets. The group above is said to be waiting to perform the Green Corn Dance, traditionally performed to celebrate the harvest after the corn was in the crib. The reductive caption for the postcard below states erroneously: "Cherokee Indians in Full Native Costume in one of their Ceremonial Dances." Even beat reporters were changing how they viewed the fair. A 1936 article in the *Knoxville Journal* gives tom-toms, moccasins, and papooses considerable coverage. (Above, Walter M. Cline, CMMHC; below, Carlos C. Campbell, CMMHC.)

THE CHEROKEE INDIAN PAGEANT, CHEROKEE, N.C.

In 1941, at the behest of Ross Cladwell, the idea of producing a reoccurring "pageant [similar to the annual event seen in the rare postcard above] concerning the history of the Cherokee in North Carolina" was first broached. The project did not gain traction, though, until 1948, when the newly formed Cherokee Historical Association settled on the outdoor drama as means to attract—and satisfy historically—visitors to the Smokies. Instead of trusting in their creative capabilities to develop the script and choreography, the historical association brought in playwright Kermit Hunter, who, in turn, sought the guidance of Harry Davis, director of the North Carolina's other outdoor drama, *The Lost Colony*. The resulting production, *Unto These Hills*, opened to audiences in the Mountainside Theatre, below, on July 1, 1950. (Above, MPC; below, Walter M. Cline, AC.)

Unto These Hills opened with the scene depicted above, "the arrival of de Soto and his Spanish Dons—first white men to visit the Cherokee," and progressed artistically to the closing scene below, "the U.S. Government's announcement to send the Cherokee from their homeland into western exile on the infamous Trail of Tears." Although liberal in its historical interpretation and inclusion of non-Cherokee performers, *Unto These Hills* offered audiences a considerably more accurate retelling of the Eastern Cherokee's history than that hawked at nearby tourist traps. The play became an instant success with audiences, and the Cherokee Historical Association was able to pay off the production's debts with the first month's ticket sales. Between 1950 and 1990, an estimated three million people witnessed the drama. Although the name remains, the script for *Unto These Hills* was rewritten in 2006. (Both, Walter M. Cline, CMMHC.)

The success of *Unto These Hills* spurred the Cherokee Historical Association to launch another history-based attraction in 1952—Oconaluftee Indian Village. Built as a 1750s village and animated by local Cherokee who demonstrated crafts and provided interpretation, the tour, according to the attraction's brochure, was to be "informal, not stereotyped." One stop on the tour, "an early Cherokee dwelling of logs," is seen here. (Walter M. Cline, AC.)

The brochure for Oconaluftee Indian Village says of the pottery demonstration: "Under an arbor of pine-boughs, the pottery-makers spin coils of clay into pots and jars. There is genius in their hands. Without potter's-wheel, [Cherokee women] turn the clay into articles of beauty and design. They are the most skilled of all Cherokee potters in the ancient technique." (Walter M. Cline, AC.)

"Later you will find [Cherokee women] working on a beaded sash for the chief," the village's brochure promises, "working with the same type of imported Venetian bead the white traders introduced into the tribe in 1750 and which supplanted the shell. Two centuries ago, such a sash ... would have been worth a fortune." (Walter M. Cline, AC.)

"Under another pine-bough arbor the basket-weavers, in their colorful and authentic costumes of homespun and calico," adds the handout, "quietly and cleverly demonstrate one of the most primitive of Indian arts. . . . Their hands are sure symphony of skill, . . . weaving baskets from both oak splits and pliable river cane." (Walter M. Cline, AC.)

Whether in search of an authentic encounter or the chance to see the Indians of the silver screen, tourists by the carloads arrived in Cherokee, and the southern gateway to the Smokies responded with the addition of businesses catering to out-of-towners. By 1954, there were 23 motor courts, 33 souvenir shops, 10 service stations, and five restaurants, all owned and operated by Cherokee. Tourist shops, like the ones above, offered the "finest selection of Indian and mountain crafts— Indian baskets, pottery, beadwork, moccasins, tomahawks, blowguns." Restaurants often attracted hungry travelers with themed gimmicks, such as the Tom-Tom Restaurant, above, or the Sequoyah Restaurant, below, which "honored" the Cherokee syllabary's creator. (Above, Gene Aiken, AC; below, AC.)

In 1965, R.B. Coburn opened Frontier Land, a Western-themed adventure park, which, given Cherokee's willingness to adopt Plains Indian trappings, seemed a natural fit. One of the park's characters, Golden Gertie, is seen here, stepping off the Butterfield Stage at Deadwood Gulch. Frontier Land's staged conflicts among the Indians and the soldiers of Fort Cherokee are long over; it is now the site of Harrah's Cherokee Casino. (AC.)

Less congruous as an attraction—but equally popular for variety-seeking tourists—was Santa's Land, opened in Cherokee by the Lyons family in 1966. At first just a North Pole–themed storybook village, the park eventually grew to have paddleboats, amusement rides, such as the Rudi-Coaster, and a petting zoo. These men are about to "see Santa's live goats" by purchasing pellets to coax the billies down from the "goat swing." (Walter M. Cline, AC.)

Five

THE HIGHLIGHT OF YOUR
MOUNTAIN TRIP!

On Monday, January 16, 1950, coonskin-capped, long rifle–armed "Slim Jim" Pryor caused a disturbance in downtown Chattanooga, Tennessee. Having garnered the attention of crowds and the law, Pryor feigned drunk on moonshine when questioned about his behavior. Just as he was about to be carted to jail, a raucous, 50-car motorcade roared through town piloted by both mountaineers and Cherokee. Signs atop the cars read, "Florida in Winter, Gatlinburg, Tenn., on Your Way Home." Pryor had been the advance party to the Travellin' Hillbillies, a publicity tour aimed at getting snowbirds to stop over in the Smokies after having wintered in Florida.

By the 1950s, luring motorists to Gatlinburg and Cherokee was as simple as spreading the word. After all, the two towns had cornered the market on the Smokies trifecta—proximity to the national park, visitor attractions that played to region's colorful history, and a wealth of modern tourist amenities.

There were other gateways—Waynesville, North Carolina, in the east, Townsend, Tennessee, in the west—but, intentionally or not, neither of these access points saw the huge influx of "fern feelers" and "flower lookers." One senses even the large cities of Asheville and Knoxville, which led the charge to open the floodgates of tourism in the region, felt bypassed by the rush of out-of-state cars.

Asheville marketed itself as "Land of the Sky" and took out advertisements, encouraging visitors "to drive on to Asheville," warning "a Smoky Mountain visit isn't complete without vacation days spent" therein. Over in Tennessee, Knoxville branded itself as the "Gateway to the Smokies." Postcards and printed pieces often emphasized the city's central location and luxurious hotels from which one could head to the mountains or to, say, Norris Lake to enjoy the by-product of a Tennessee Valley Authority dam.

For Ashevillians and Knoxvillians, distance made the impact of tourism less immediate, but few today would decry the lasting advantages brought to their cities by the establishment of Great Smoky Mountains National Park.

At the heart of the "Land of the Sky" was the bustling city of Asheville, fittingly seen here from an aerial view. In its attempt to lure visitors to Great Smoky Mountains National Park on over to Western North Carolina's capital city, another postcard offers the following lines of reasoning: "Mountain air is the cleanest / Heaven is the nearest / Friendships are the dearest / In Asheville. / Water is the purest / Summer skies are the bluest / And mosquitoes are the fewest / In Asheville. / Maidens are the fairest / Flowers are the rarest / Businessmen the squarest / In Asheville. / Flappers are the boldest / Sunshine is the goldest / And people live the oldest / In Asheville. / Sportsman are the gamest / Bachelors are the tamest / And kickers are the lamest / In Asheville. / Streets are the cleanest / Realtors are the keenest / 'And moonshine is the meanest' / In Asheville." (CMMHC.)

When Edwin W. Grove first visited Asheville in the mid-1890s, it was to take in "the cure" of the cool mountain air. Grove, though, recognized the city's potential as a pleasure resort, so in 1913, he opened the Grove Park Inn, "the finest resort hotel in the world . . . for tired people who are not sick." The inn quickly became a favorite of wealthy tourists, who often gathered in the Big Room, or lobby, above, which could "comfortably entertain 1,000 people." In the 1920s, Grove pushed his tourist-based speculations in Asheville further, razing a Victorian hotel and building a modern convention center, the Battery Park Hotel, below, in its place. At the time, it seemed Asheville was positioning itself to be the Smokies preeminent gateway. (Both, CMMHC.)

In 1888, George W. Vanderbilt chose Asheville for his opulent estate, Biltmore (pictured). In 1931, as the park service was taking over jurisdiction in the Smokies, Asheville welcomed tourists into America's largest home for the first time. Even though some questioned opening an attraction that displayed such wealth amid the Great Depression, Biltmore eventually became the regional draw it remains today. (CMMHC.)

"Although the Asheville Chamber had been ardent supporters of the park movement," notes tourism scholar C. Breneden Martin, "the national park drew more tourists away from rather than to Asheville." Scenic highways, such as US 19 and US 23 crossing Great Smoky Mountains Bridge over the French Broad River (pictured), funneled motorists past Asheville toward the closer and cheaper accommodations of Gatlinburg and Cherokee. (CMMHC.)

Although distance may have hampered Asheville's and Knoxville's gains in the tourist industry when compared to closer gateways, both cities continued to use the Smokies to their advantage. The caption for this postcards reads: "America's most popular park can be crossed by through bus service running between Knoxville . . . and Asheville. . . . Ask your agent to route your trip through the heart of the Great Smoky Mountains National Park on comfortable Trailways buses." (CMMHC.)

TUSCULUM COLLEGE, GREENEVILLE, TENN.—9
"GATEWAY TO THE GREAT SMOKY MOUNTAINS"

Small communities wanted a piece of the Smokies pie, too. On this postcard, Tennessee's oldest college, Tusculum College, and the nearby town of Greeneville proclaim themselves to be "Gateway to the Great Smoky Mountains." The sender of this postcard, though, says of the Smokies, "This is the way they look on a clear day, only we don't see so much of them from here." (AC.)

Down the road from Gatlinburg and through Pigeon Forge sits Sevierville—Sevier County's seat and legitimate heir to becoming a gateway to Great Smoky Mountains National Park. "Many tourists each year make their headquarters in Sevierville," reports one travel brochure, "because of the city conveniences, police and fire protection, and the reasonable rates for food and lodging." The report adds, "No advance or 'hold-up' prices are tolerated for tourists." The postcard above shows Chapman Highway, named in honor of park movement leader Col. David Chapman, approaching Sevierville from Knoxville. The postcard below emphasizes Sevierville's proximity to the mountains. (Both, CMMHC.)

Seemingly everyone in Knoxville—from community leaders to schoolchildren—had given of himself or herself to see Great Smoky Mountains National Park created, and advertisements in the 1920s and 1930s show the city's determination to simultaneously remain close to the Smokies story and profit from the region's other tourist offerings. Using a cynosure's move, the caption for the above postcard leads the viewer to believe this view of Mount Le Conte can be had "near Knoxville," when in reality, one would need to be standing above Gatlinburg. The golden arrow in the card below more accurately posits Knoxville in its hoped-for role, smack dab between the "greatest inland waterway" of Norris Lake and The Loop on US 441 in Great Smoky Mountains National Park. (Above, James E. Thompson, BBBC; below, AC.)

Knoxville's hoteliers followed suit in their promotions. The Andrew Johnson Hotel, the tall building on the left in the postcard above, ran advertisements encouraging visitors to "enjoy modern comfort and city amusements, then make side trips daily through the mountain region. From the Andrew Johnson it is only an hour's drive to Gatlinburg, entrance to the Great Smoky Mountains National Park, and even less to Norris Lake." Likewise, Knoxville's Hotel St. James, below, offered air-cooled, fireproof rooms right between the black bears of the mountains and the crystal clear lake impounded by Norris Dam. (Above, CMMHC; below, AC.)

Just the evocation of the name "Great Smoky Mountains" was becoming a powerful draw. The roadside accommodation, above, was located closer to Knoxville than the mountains but recognized the benefits of being known as the Smoky Mt. Tourist Court. Even Land's Drive In on Knoxville's urban Magnolia Avenue chose to use three of its six pictures on the postcard below to highlight black bears, Chimney Tops, and Mount Le Conte—all 38 miles away. Apparently, these Smokies images were more alluring than photographs of the drive-in's hamburgers, milkshakes, and fries. (Both, CMMHC.)

While Knoxville and other towns, such as the self-proclaimed "sportsman's mecca" of LaFollette, Tennessee, promoted Norris Lake, man-made lakes in North Carolina provided visitors to Great Smoky Mountains another outlet for recreation, just beyond park boundaries. Mountain dams, such as Santeetlah, above, and Calderwood, below, were built on the Little Tennessee and Cheoha Rivers, beginning in the late 1910s, to provide flood control and power for the Aluminum Corporation of America's (ALCOA) smelting and rolling operations in Alcoa, Tennessee. These North Carolina dams, though, paled in comparison to the imposing, 480-foot tall Fontana Dam—the tallest in the eastern United States—built by the Tennessee Valley Authority (TVA) at the height of World War II. (Both, CMMHC.)

Fontana Dam, right, was TVA's massive public works effort to provide ALCOA with enough energy to meet the aluminum demands of war. When the gates of the $70-million dam closed on November 11, 1944, more than 6,000 people had worked on-site, many housed in a camp called Welch Cove, later Fontana Village. In 1946, TVA leased Fontana Village to an outside company for repurposing as a Smokies resort community. Bel Airs and Fairlanes replaced work trucks, as a cafeteria, at left below, and a drugstore and gift shop, in the distance below, replaced mess halls and administrative buildings. Fontana Village still operates today, a popular spot for hikers on the Appalachian Trail to regroup before setting out on the next leg. (Right, AC; below, Walter M. Cline, AC.)

The 2,115 miles of rocky streams in Great Smoky Mountains National Park offered outdoor enthusiasts essentially two options, either trout fishing or wading. With the creation of the mountain lakes and other nearby TVA lakes, such as Norris, Douglas, and Cherokee, sportsmen were able to combine a trip to the Smokies with other activities, including motorboating, water-skiing, and bass fishing. Smooth waterways also facilitated canoeing, as the boys at summer camp demonstrate (above), or simply relaxing dockside (below). Recently, some unimpounded rivers on the park's edge have become favorites of white-water rafters and kayakers. (Both, CMMHC.)

Six

Y'ALL COME BACK

In 1982, longtime Gatlinburg resident Lucinda Oakley Ogle remarked, "They laugh at me making pigs out of bottles. . . . But, I tell them I've sent two kids to college selling those pigs to people that think they're mountain crafts." As promised by regional boosters, Great Smoky Mountains National Park brought profit to mountain communities through the wallets of pleasure-seekers.

In the formative years of the park, the emphasis on profit often pitted boosters against the increasingly cautious and preservation-minded National Park Service. In 1935, for instance, the Great Smoky Mountains Conservation Association, eager to make the park "more attractive," proposed, among other things, erecting an electric sign stating, "Welcome to Mankind," and transforming Cades Cove into a lake by damming Abrams Creek. In 1938, to squelch these improvements, Arno Cammerer, director of the National Park Service, resurrected an argument used previously to defeat the proposed skyline drive, stating this "sort of installation [should] be supplied outside the boundaries."

"Outside the boundaries," Gatlinburg, Pigeon Forge, and later Sevierville witnessed, and continue to see, radical development. Although some criticized this tsunami of change, there was something special about the first wave: it was local. Families with generations-old ties to the land paced building projects in Gatlinburg and often lent their personalities to tourist amenities. Love them or hate them, hillbilly diversions, such as Hillbilly Golf and Hee Haw Village, were rooted in local lore. And, even as late as 1986, when Sevier County native Dolly Parton rebranded a Pigeon Forge theme park, she saw the benefit of hawking "homespun fun."

Over the years, as the whims of the millions of visitors who continue to flock to the Smokies have changed, some of the area's vernacular hospitality and fun has been replaced with chain establishments. It seems "anywhere America" is now taking root. The vintage postcards of the Smokies and the stories they evoke remind one, though, that it was not sameness but uniqueness— the individuality and shared beauty of the mountains and their people—that made the area attractive, worthy of preserving the "nation's greatest pleasure ground," Great Smoky Mountains National Park.

Founded during the first years of the 1800s, White Oak Flats became Gatlinburg in 1856, apparently at the behest of Radford Gatlin, who opened a post office at his general store that year. By the 1910s, as Pi Beta Phi's settlement school was getting underway, Gatlinburg, as pictured, remained a small mountain community with six houses, three general stores, and a church. Most families lived on nearby farms. (CMMHC.)

Exponential growth came to Gatlinburg with the establishment of Great Smoky Mountains National Park. The park service chose the town for its headquarters, and so did tourists. During the late 1930s to the early 1940s, the Parkway, seen here, began to be lined with hotels, gift shops, and gas stations. Rattlesnake Ridge looms in the distance, the Edgepark Inn is at left, and the Cliff Dwellers Shop is at right. (CMMHC.)

By 1942, about the time this aerial view was taken, the number of buildings in Gatlinburg had skyrocketed to 641. The count jumped to 1,114 in 1956, and the number of businesses doubled. By 1963, the year 5.2 million people entered the national park, visitors could avail themselves of 47 restaurants, 153 motels, and 73 swimming pools. (Walter M. Cline, CMMHC.)

In 1916, when he opened the Mountain View Hotel, Andy Huff launched the hospitality industry in Gatlinburg. At that time, his guests were wealthy businessmen, but by the 1940s, when this postcard was printed, motor-touring, middle-class Americans overran this "pioneer hostelry," making it "the ideal base for full enjoyment of the unexcelled beauties and unlimited recreational areas of the Great Smoky Mountains National Park." (Paul A. Moore, CMMHC.)

561—Hotel Greystone, Gatlinburg, Tenn.
"Entrance to Great Smoky Mountains National Park"

Steve Whaley sold his apple orchard on Bullhead Mountain in 1925 and entered Gatlinburg's hospitality arena, building the Riverside Hotel. In 1941, the Whaleys added more overnight accommodations with the Hotel Greystone (pictured). The Huffs, Whaleys, and Ogles owned a major share of the land in Gatlinburg, and they quickly found themselves to be influential decision makers. In fact, Steve's son Dick Whaley became the city of Gatlinburg's first mayor. (BBBC.)

The Gatlinburg Inn was the city's third major resort, opening in 1939. Under the direction of R.L. "Rellie" Maples and his wife, Wilma, the inn hosted not only notable events—Gatlinburg's first bank, newspaper, and city offices were all organized there—but also notable guests, including, among others, "Lady Bird" Johnson, Liberace, Dinah Shore, J.C. Penney, and Tennessee Ernie Ford. In Room 388, Felice and Boudleaux Bryant penned Tennessee's anthem, "Rocky Top." (Walter M. Cline, CMMHC.)

Not all lodging in Gatlinburg was to be had at the large resorts. Those looking for a more rustic or informal experience could avail themselves of automobile camps, such as Perry's Camp on the Little Pigeon River (above), or tourist courts, such as Bohanan's Tourist Rooms and Cabins (below), which offered "17 units, tub and shower." No matter the level of accommodation, word was spreading that Gatlinburg was the place for mountain hospitality. One travel writer reported, "The new Gatlinburg, conscious that it has a precious inheritance to share with touring Americans, has modernized its facilities for feeding and housing guests." (Above, Walter M. Cline, CMMHC; below, Walter M. Cline, AC.)

Catering to the realization that if tourists needed a place to sleep they would also require a place to eat, restaurants began to open in profusion in Gatlinburg. Cafeterias and buffets were popular. Pancakes were—and continue to reign—supreme. "Our food is prepared by native cooks," proclaimed one hillbilly-themed advertisement for crowd-favorite Ogle's Cafe, "Good mountain vittuls cooked by mountaineers!" Blanche D. Moffett, owner of the M&O Tea Room (above), promised her establishment was "the home of good food." Diners passed a "ye olde wishing well" on the way into the refined restaurant. For those on the way into the park, there were places, like Anderson's Food Market (below), where a hot dog and RC Cola or supplies for a picnic could be easily had. (Above, CMMHC; below, AC.)

Gatlinburg Ski Resort, seen here from the top of the intermediate slope on Mount Harrison, opened in 1961, as a seasonal draw. To take advantage of warm-weather tourists, the ski resort was retooled as Ober Gatlinburg in 1975 and began encouraging visitors to take the Aerial Tramway "to the mountain of family fun" year-round. (Walter M. Cline, CMMHC.)

Built in 380 days, Gatlinburg's 342-foot-tall Space Needle opened to tourists wanting to get a better view of Gatlinburg in 1970. The all-steel, four-million-pound tower transports visitors to the observation deck via two elevators that can travel up to 453 feet per minute. At the base of the Space Needle, the staunchly pro-Confederate Rebel Corner sold wares to Southern sympathizers, until it was destroyed by fire in 1992. (Walter M. Cline, AC.)

Tourist attractions sprang up in other small towns near Great Smoky Mountains National Park but not with the initial concentration and lasting success experienced by Gatlinburg. Just beyond Cherokee, North Carolina, travelers on US 19 were told, "Howdy!" by a painted sign depicting Maggie, a sun-bonneted figure who "sez, 'You are now entering Maggie Valley, elevation 4,000 feet.'" For Maggie Valley, above, the star attraction was Ghost Town in the Sky, below, one of a handful of frontier-inspired theme parks founded by R.B. Coburn. After purchasing tickets, guests were whisked to Ghost Town in the Sky either by a chairlift or by a bus for those whose stomachs were not up to the open-air lift. (Both, AC.)

When Ghost Town in the Sky opened in June 1961, one could "walk side by side with gunfighters and marshals. Witness the dramatic shootout between the sheriff, bank robbers, and outlaws. See Indians perform ritual war dances. Relax with singing and dancing at the Red Baron Saloon." The next two decades saw the addition of an amusement area with the oft-touted inverted roller coaster (above) and "more than 20 of your favorite rides" (below). R.B. Coburn sold Ghost Town in the Sky in the early 1980s only to buy it back a few years later to save it from demise. The park was eventually shuttered in 2002, and although there have been recent attempts to revive the attraction, the absence of Ghost Town in the Sky has dealt a major blow to the tourism industry in Maggie Valley. (Both, AC.)

Tuckaleechee Village
Townsend, Tenn.

By the time lumber operations were coming to a close in Townsend in the late 1930s, Gatlinburg had already cornered the market on handicrafts and hospitality. It appears, though, that the western gateway to Great Smoky Mountains National Park took advantage of what it lacked and began touting itself, as it does today, as the "Peaceful Side of the Smokies." In their captioning, postcards, like the one above for Dock's Cabins, emphasize not modern amenities but "swimming, hiking, and fishing." Even Tuckaleechee Village, left, described its property as "restful" and "relaxing" before noting "ultra modern cabins." As an interesting aside, Col. W.C. Taylor and his wife, the owners of Tuckaleechee Village, sent this postcard to *The Price Is Right*'s Holiday Showcase sweepstakes in 1957 with a bid of $6,190.61. (Above, BBBC; left, CMMHC.)

Peaceful did not mean that Townsend was devoid of attractions. In 1953, W.E. "Bill" Vananda and Harry Myers opened Tuckaleechee Caverns as the "Greatest Sight Under the Smokies." Here is a view of stalagmites in the Big Room, the largest cavern room in the East, measuring 500 feet long, 300 feet wide, and 150 feet high. The caverns attracted 2,000 visitors during its first year of operation. (Frank Shannon, AC.)

Nor did peaceful mean that Townsend was devoid of hillbilly marketing. John and Norma Wilson used Li'l Abner–esque cutouts to decorate the front of their restaurant and hotel, both of which were "recommended by Cousin Clem." Apparently, Cousin Clem found the Wilson's "ham steaks from mt. hawgs, fride chiken, ho-made bread, two," to be desirable. For a time, Townsend would also be home to the Hillbilly Hilton. (CMMHC.)

State Sanitation Grade "A" RESTAURANT – MOTEL

Eat with the WILSONS!

MT. HAWG STEAKS

Ho-Made BREAD

MT. FRIDE CHICKEN

XXX FLOUR

XXX CORN

NORMA   JOHN

THE WILSON'S RESTAURANT & MOTEL

Located Between Gatlinburg & Maryville on Smoky Mountain Highway 73
Mailing address: Box 29, Townsend, Tennessee

With Gatlinburg established as a tourist hub, nearby Pigeon Forge, above, began to experience similar rapid change. "Still growing today," opines a 1968 press release, "Pigeon Forge has everything to offer the tourist: 21 fine motels, . . . six Grade A restaurants, . . . and an endless array of tourist attractions and entertainment." Pigeon Forge is "still growing today," and as Tim Hollis notes, "It sometimes seems that approximately the same number of businesses can [now] be found in a one-block area of Pigeon Forge." One of the tourist attractions that started it all is the Old Mill on the Little Pigeon River, seen at left in the above postcard and in detail below. Built in 1830, the mill has remained in continuous operation and is now part of a large, restaurant–gift shop complex. (Above, Walter M. Cline, CMMHC; below, Frank Shannon, CMMHC.)

In 1946, Douglas Ferguson, seen here at his potter's wheel, and his wife, Ruth, opened Pigeon Forge Pottery not far from the Old Mill. A former employee of the Tennessee Valley Authority's Ceramic Research Laboratory at Norris, Douglas Ferguson praised the native clay, a rich, dark red clay found about a mile from the pottery. (Gene Aiken, CMMHC.)

Pigeon Forge Pottery became an early and favorite attraction for tourists. The sign, which proclaimed, "See It Made," helped attract passing cars, but so did Cyclone Jim, the horse that powered the clay-grinding mill in front of the pottery. "Glazes made from minerals gathered in the Great Smoky Mountains lend to the local clay rich shades of color rarely found elsewhere," notes the pottery's brochure. (ETHSC.)

"All designs and creative works are done by Pigeon Forge craftsmen," adds Pigeon Forge Pottery's handout. "Designs are inspired by native subjects and materials. Only native talented craftsmen are employed and carefully trained to help make the very special line of gift ware." One of those lines was the pottery's black bears, seen as bisque ware in the foreground. (Walter M. Cline, CMMHC.)

Hillbillies built a "village" in Pigeon Forge around 1954. Here, out-of-towners could peel off US 441 and find the obligatory moonshine still and cabin required of such attractions. Souvenirs in profusion could also be had at Hill-Billy Village, which this postcard lists as including "Indian and hand made hillbilly dolls, tom toms, mt. honey, and woven purses, towels, and woven rugs. Over 10,000 items." (Walter M. Cline, AC.)

The self-proclaimed "exciting—educational" Fort Weare Game Park sat near, as this postcard explains, the original Fort Weare, "named in honor of Colonel Samuel Wear, pioneer of Tennessee, and soldier of four wars, Colonial, Revolution, Indian, and 1812." Perhaps this detail helps explain how the Miller brothers settled on the idea of presenting in Pigeon Forge "the finest of nature's specimens of wild life . . . shown in an authentic pioneer atmosphere." Inside the fort, visitors strolled through animal exhibits, played at the petting zoo, watched trained animals perform, such as Judy the India elephant (pictured), and perused displays of pioneer and Cherokee artifacts. Fort Weare asked of its guests: "It will be much appreciated if you will show this folder to a friend back home who might later be traveling this way also." (Above, AC; right, CMMHC.)

Judy - Trained India Elephant - Fort Weare - Pigeon Forge, Tenn.   1-1-481

Sometime around 1958, Margaret Swan of Knoxville bought this Pigeon Forge attraction, Fairyland, from its original owner, who must have found merit in mixing the plots of children's fairy tales. Visitors observed the juxtaposed scenes through windows and then sped off to the "merry-go-round and speed boats on water" that were also offered. (Thompsons, AC.)

A 1915 Model T Ford, known as "Copperhead," sits in front of the Smoky Mountain Car Museum, which exhibited automobiles so rare they were not to be "found displayed in [the] Smithsonian Institution, Washington, D. C." The museum's collection, which opened to the public in 1956, grew to include cars from Hollywood movies and notable figures, such as McNairy County, Tennessee, lawman Buford Pusser. (Gene Aiken, CMMHC.)

In 1968, East Tennessee's beloved Grand Ole Opry star Archie Campbell launched a stage show called *Stars of the Grand Ole Opry* at Gatlinburg's Heritage Hall. A decade later, the show's blend of music, dance, and comedy had become so popular, the act had to be moved to Gatlinburg's Ramada Inn Convention Center and soon thereafter to Archie Campbell's Hee Haw Village, a miniature theme park in Pigeon Forge based on the popular television show. Other acts took off, too. Bonnie Lou and Buster packed the Pigeon Forge Coliseum with their *Smoky Mountain Hayride.* Bill and Kathy Owens and the Boogertown Boogie Band stocked the Smoky Mountain Music Barn, below. The foundation had been laid for the massive expansion of music and variety theaters that would occur, especially in Pigeon Forge, in the 1990s. (Above, Creed, AC; below, Walter M. Cline, AC.)

Building on their success with the Tweetsie Railroad near Blowing Rock, North Carolina, the Robbins brothers decided to try their hand at a similar, train-based attraction in Pigeon Forge, Tennessee. Playing to the Civil War's centennial, the Robbins brothers landed on the idea of Rebel Railroad, wherein guests became visitors to the 1860 Rebeltown and participant in the raid on the Union's Fort Agony. (ETHSC.)

With the Civil War's centennial wearing thin by 1964, the Robbins brothers looked for another way to rebrand Rebel Railroad. They settled on Goldrush Junction, a return to the familiar frontier-style town attraction, and soon Confederates were replaced with forty-niners. The Iron Mountain Tavern anchored Goldrush Junction, where, as this postcard reports, "Talent scouts realize the finest young performers in the Southeast are presented on stage." (Gene Aiken, CMMHC.)

The change to Goldrush Junction brought the park's first amusement ride—this log flume, which had originally operated at the 1964–1965 New York World's Fair. In 1970, the Robbins brothers sold the theme park to the Cleveland Browns football team, who by 1976 had transferred ownership to Jack and Pete Herschend, operators of Silver Dollar City in Branson, Missouri. In 1977, the Herschends changed Goldrush Junction's image again, this time to Silver Dollar City. (AC.)

Under the Herschends' direction, Silver Dollar City began playing to local mountain crafts and heritage. When Sevier County's own Dolly Parton announced on television that she wanted to build a theme park somewhere in Pigeon Forge, the Herschends smartly—and quickly—offered Parton part ownership. Silver Dollar City became Dollywood in 1986, "homespun fun" continued to be emphasized, and, as is often said, the rest is history. (AC.)

For those who truly cherish the Great Smoky Mountains, one trip into the ancient hills is never enough. Repeated and prolonged stays were at the heart of those who enjoyed the mountains from their summer cottages at Elkmont. To take in the breadth and grandeur of the Smokies, members of the Southern Appalachian National Park Committee had to make more than one exploratory trip. Descendants of families who gave up their mountain homes now return annually for homecomings. Organizations that support the National Park Service's efforts through fundraising, such as the Great Smoky Mountains Conservation Association, Great Smoky Mountains Association, and Friends of the Smokies, are made up of members who cannot get enough of—or give enough to—the national park. And, even some casual tourists, who use Great Smoky Mountains National Park as an excuse to participate in the entertainment meccas that are Cherokee, Gatlinburg, Pigeon Forge, and Sevierville, make a trip to the mountains an annual pilgrimage. Perhaps the lure of the Smokies is, then, the repeated entreaty "Y'all come back." (Oscar N. Wilson, CMMHC.)

BIBLIOGRAPHY

Adams, Paul J. *Mt. LeConte*. Self-published, 1966.

Beard-Moose, Christina Taylor. *Public Indians, Private Cherokees: Tourism and Tradition on Tribal Ground*. Tuscaloosa: University of Alabama Press, 2009.

Brown, Margaret Lynn. *The Wild East: A Biography of the Great Smoky Mountains*. Gainesville: University Press of Florida, 2000.

Campbell, Carlos C. *Birth of a National Park in the Great Smoky Mountains*. Knoxville: University of Tennessee Press, 1960.

Coggins, Allen R. *Place Names of the Smokies*. Gatlinburg, TN: Great Smoky Mountains Natural History Association, 1999.

Cotham, Steve. *The Great Smoky Mountains National Park*. Charleston, SC: Arcadia Publishing, 2006.

Dunn, Durwood. *Cades Cove: The Life and Death of a Southern Appalachian Community 1818–1937*. Knoxville: University of Tennessee Press, 1988.

Dykeman, Wilma and Jim Stokely. *Mountain Home: A Pictorial History of Great Smoky Mountains National Park*. Gatlinburg, TN: Great Smoky Mountains Natural History Association, 2009.

Frome, Michael. *Strangers in High Places: The Story of the Great Smoky Mountains*. Knoxville: University of Tennessee Press, 1980.

Hollis, Tim. *The Land of the Smokies: Great Mountain Memories*. Jackson: University Press of Mississippi, 2007.

Kephart, Horace. *Our Southern Highlanders: A Narrative of Adventure in the Southern Appalachians and a Study of Life among the Mountaineers*. Knoxville: University of Tennessee Press, 1976.

Martin, C. Brenden. *Tourism in the Mountain South: A Double-Edged Sword*. Knoxville: University of Tennessee Press, 2007.

Pierce, Daniel S. *The Great Smokies: From Natural Habitat to National Park*. Knoxville: University of Tennessee Press, 2000.

Thornborough, Laura. *The Great Smoky Mountains*. Knoxville: University of Tennessee Press, 1937.

Weals, Vic. *Last Train to Elkmont: A Look Back at Life on Little River in the Great Smoky Mountains*. Knoxville, TN: Olden Press, 1991.

DISCOVER THOUSANDS OF LOCAL HISTORY BOOKS FEATURING MILLIONS OF VINTAGE IMAGES

Arcadia Publishing, the leading local history publisher in the United States, is committed to making history accessible and meaningful through publishing books that celebrate and preserve the heritage of America's people and places.

Find more books like this at
www.arcadiapublishing.com

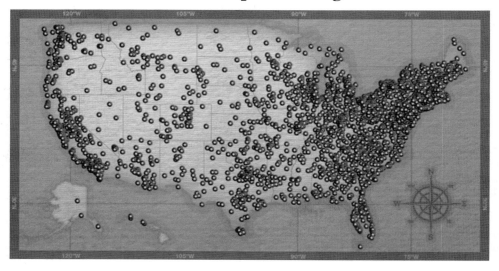

Search for your hometown history, your old stomping grounds, and even your favorite sports team.